Tutoring:

Learning by Helping

(Revised Edition)

by

Elizabeth Sabrinsky Foster

A Student Handbook for

Training Peer and Cross-Age Tutors

Appreciation

It is hard to thank people who have made a book possible. There's always someone left out that shouldn't be or words put together less meaningfully than intended. With that in mind I want to try and share my gratitude.

My biggest thanks to all my students, colleagues, and friends, who wanted to be part of a "vision" in education. Thanks to a tolerant and adventuresome faculty at Manteo High School. A big thank you to all of the people who have used this book and sent notes or let me know what worked and what did not. For believing there could be more for students and for believing in me—thanks to Dr. Norman Sprinthall.

Copyright 1983, 1992

EDUCATIONAL MEDIA CORPORATION®
P.O. Box 21311
Minneapolis, Minnesota 55421
(612)-781-0088

Library of Congress Catalog Card No. 92-071011
ISBN 0-932796-44-3
Revised 1992, Fifth Printing
Printing - (last digit)

15 14 13 12 10 9 8 7 6

Blank forms may be duplicated for use with your classes only. The remainder of this book may not be reproduced or used in any form without the expressed permission of the publisher in writing. Manufactured in the United States of America.

Production editor—
   Don L. Sorenson
Graphic design—
   Earl Sorenson
Illustrator—
   Mary M. McKee

Table of Contents

Chapter 1
   Orientation to Tutoring 1

Chapter 2
   Developing Helping Relationships
   in Tutoring 19

Chapter 3
   Communication Skills 25

Chapter 4
   Establishing Proper Behavior
   in Tutoring 45

Chapter 5
   Principles of Education as Applied
   in Tutoring 55

Chapter 6
   Roles, Responsibilities and Procedures
   in Tutoring 63

Chapter 7
   Content Area Instruction
   Through Tutoring 77

Chapter 8
   Recordkeeping Functions in Tutoring 115

Chapter 9
   Evaluation in Tutoring 125

Appendix 132

About the Author 135

A Note to Students 135

A Note To Leaders 136

Acknowledgments 136

Selected References 137

Code of Ethics for Peer Helpers
   National Peer Helpers Association 140

Foreword to Students

Welcome to the world of peer *tutoring*. You will learn many new things and find this a challenging job as well as a rewarding experience. Part of the fun in learning is discovering new things. That is just what you are about to do. You will discover some very important things about yourself as well as about other people with whom you will work. You will find that working with others can bring out the best in you.

This handbook is a guide to prepare you for the weeks and months ahead. Each chapter in this book is designed to help you strengthen your ability to tutor; specifically in communication, relating, management, recordkeeping and evaluation skills. The training activities will increase your awareness of your strengths and weaknesses. We all possess both. Successful people are willing to look at all of their strengths and build upon them, thereby decreasing the weaknesses. It is never too late to learn. It is never too late to improve. It is our job to provide successfully quality help to those who request it.

As a peer helper, you will be expected to assume responsibility not often offered to students. With this responsibility comes the challenge for you to provide not only knowledge, but a bit of yourself, as well. This responsibility will open unique opportunities in the school. Keep in mind that the training activities and the training program is designed to help you be your best and to allow you to make a difference for someone else, as well as for yourself.

Educational Media Corporation®, Box 21311, Minneapolis, MN 55421-0311

Overview of Tutoring

What is tutoring?

Tutoring is a supplemental service program designed to aid the teacher, the tutor, and the student receiving the tutoring service. Though the peer helper concept has been around a long time, utilization of student energy and skill is often an overlooked resource.

What are the advantages of being a tutor?

There are many advantages for students who want to become tutors. Tutors learn a great deal about themselves and develop a sense of identity through their role in education. Tutoring develops a sense of responsibility, a tolerance for and an understanding of individual differences/needs, and a sensitivity toward the learning process. Tutoring encourages an awareness of self and develops the skills to deal with others. Tutoring provides practice in time management, behavior management, and record management. To sum it up, tutoring will benefit the tutor in the following ways:

1. Increases self awareness
2. Develops a positive self-image
3. Creates a sensitivity and tolerance for individual needs and differences
4. Develops positive attitudes toward school, instructors and education
5. Improves skill development and academic achievement
6. Develops a sense of responsibility
7. Encourages wise use of time, behavior and records

What training is involved?

An integral part of the tutoring program is the tutor training. Tutor training involves the following: Orientation to Tutoring, Developing Helping Relationships in Tutoring, Communication Skills, Behavior Management, Principles of Education as Applied in Tutoring, Roles, Responsibilities and Procedures in Tutoring, How to Tutor in Content Areas, Recordkeeping, and Evaluation Tools. The optimal training period is a nine-week block of time; however, training periods of a different duration can also be used. Training should continue throughout the year after the initial block of training.

The on-going training can be continued through a variety of methods. One such method is through a teacher-tutor in-service approach. Once per nine weeks, student tutors receive training with their supervising or receiving instructors, off the school campus (on the campus sometimes can also be as effective) for a concentrated four- to six-hour session. Local or outside consultants can be utilized to provide training on such topics as motivation, problem solving, and goal setting.

The second method of training, which should be included with the concentrated training session, is through the regularly scheduled class meeting time. Tutors would continue to meet for on-going, on-the-job training designed to strengthen their tutoring skills. These meetings would occur once per week or once every two weeks at a minimum.

The opportunity to receive feedback on tutoring experiences would occur at this time. Time to develop new skills or to refine those that are currently being practiced should also be provided.

Training in tutoring is a new world of learning. It should be exciting and create a desire in you to know more about yourself and your friends. Analyze the purpose of each lesson and reflect with your fellow students on how the concepts apply to the actual process of tutoring.

Chapter 1
Orientation to Tutoring

Chapter Concepts:

1. The process of education involves the development of mind, body, expression and emotion.
2. Self-concept affects everything you do.
3. Knowing and understanding yourself helps you to better interact with others.

Chapter Objectives:

1. To help you to discover the qualities which make you unique and special.
2. To help you to learn the responsibilities of working with others while strengthening your self-image.

Chapter Description:

This chapter is an introduction to the peer tutoring concept. This material will help you to learn more about yourself so you will be aware of your personal strengths and weaknesses. You must understand yourself and your motives for being a tutor before you begin to work with other people. After completing the orientation chapter, you will build upon your strengths to develop a tutoring relationship with another student.

Chapter Vocabulary:

goal, rapport, secluded, performance level, relevant, audio visual, characteristic, tutee, expectations, psychological, clarification

Contents

1.01	Thinking Ahead	Reading Selection	2
1.02	Education	Reading Selection	3
1.03	Tutoring Pre-Test	Activity	4
1.04	So You Want to be a Tutor	Reading Selection	5
1.05	Who is the Tutee?	Reading Selection	6
1.06	Success or Failure Questionnaire	Activity	7
1.07	Being Real	Reading Selection	8
1.08	Success and Being Real	Reading Selection	9
1.09	The Animal School	Activity	9
1.10	Circle Gram	Activity	12
1.11	Motivation and Needs	Reading Selection	14
1.12	Self-Effectiveness Chart	Activity	16
1.13	Self-Effectiveness Analysis	Follow-up Exercise	17
1.14	It's Tough Being Human	Activity	17
1.15	It's Tough Being Human-Look Again	Follow-up Exercise	18
1.16	What is This Thing Called Confidentiality?	Reading Activity	18

1.01 Reading Selection

Thinking Ahead

Purpose:

To encourage you, the tutor, to "think ahead."

Directions:

Read and discuss the following:

Thinking ahead... but maybe of now
and how you'll do it all....
All those things everyone else
says will help you "later."
The later you could-or would
never see, but for the
REMINDERS. . . ."Just wait."
Why wait?
Do "something" now.
Maybe it WILL help later—maybe now—
maybe you, maybe someone else—
Maybe you are thinking ahead?

Discussion Questions:

1. Why is it important to think ahead when you are working with another person?
2. What difficulties do you encounter as a planner?
3. What are the characteristics that make someone a good planner?

1.02 Reading Selection
Education

Purpose:
To provide an overview of education and its relationship to tutoring.

Directions:
Read and discuss the following definitions:

Education is the joining of thoughts and ideas to form concepts and principles from which we can make judgments and wise decisions.

Education is the process of broadening the whole mind and whole body to assure that horizons are limitless.

Education is the opportunity to explore social, intellectual, emotional, moral and psychological aspects of the individual and society as a whole to attain a personal code of ethics upon which daily life should be based.

Education is thinking ahead so the behind isn't in front.

These definitions of education could all be considered valid. Some people might wish to add or delete parts to those definitions. The lack of agreement on what education should be has led to many different approaches to learning.

Those who feel that education is something that happens only in an individual's brain fail to consider the learner's motives and emotions. Learning involves much more than just ingesting information. Processing information and applying it to life require the learner to call upon past and present resources of feeling, thinking, interaction, and social development to process properly and to transfer the information.

We must not separate the mind from the spirit, the mind from feeling, and the mind from social development as we determine how to best teach and learn. True education involves sharing and caring and encourages the total growth of an individual. Those concepts are entwined eternally in the preservation of mankind, for which education is intended.

Education in all its many forms promotes the ability of young people to deal with each other and those around them in a sharing-caring atmosphere. The root of mankind is nourished through caring; it survives through sharing.

Discussion Questions:
1. How do you think education can promote the ability of young people to relate to each other?
2. What can schools do to encourage students to care and share?
3. How important in life is it to be able to "relate" to people?
4. How does your school promote "sharing and caring?"

1.03 Activity
Tutoring Pre-Test

Purpose:
To provide information on the student's perceptions of tutoring.

Directions:
Respond to each of the following statements by circling A for **Always**, B for **Sometimes**, and C for **Never** to best describe how you feel about each statement. A=Always, B=Sometimes, C=Never

A B C 1. It is necessary to have some pre-established goals for each student during tutoring sessions.

A B C 2. It is necessary to have a quiet, secluded, attractive area in which to tutor.

A B C 3. It is always necessary to know something about the student being tutored when making plans to meet that student's individual needs.

A B C 4. It is advisable to encourage the student who is being tutored to work on tasks which are just beyond that student's performance level.

A B C 5. It is desirable to maintain a calm voice if you must reprimand a student you are tutoring.

A B C 6. It is important that you keep accurate, up-to-date records of each tutoring session.

A B C 7. In trying to establish rapport with a student, it is helpful to be friendly, interested, encouraging, and considerate.

A B C 8. It is helpful to the teacher and student if you are familiar with the materials you will be using.

A B C 9. Your attitude toward learning does influence the student's attitude toward learning.

A B C 10. You should try to have the student with whom you are working leave each tutoring session with a feeling of success.

A B C 11. It is important to make the learning activities interesting and relevant.

A B C 12. The tutoring session should be designed to meet the student's learning style and rate.

A B C 13. It would be helpful to know something about the student's hobbies, family, friends and academic strengths and weaknesses.

A B C 14. Using audio-visual equipment to demonstrate a skill is more helpful and practical than using a book or chalkboard.

A B C 15. It is possible to determine when a student no longer needs your assistance.

A B C 16. It is helpful to use a variety of materials and activities to help the student reinforce a newly acquired skill.

A B C 17. A tutor can be effective with a particular student even if the tutor disagrees with the approach the student's teacher is using in the classroom.

A B C 18. It is advisable to begin the first tutoring session with a test to see what the student does know.

A B C 19. The student will benefit from the tutoring session if the student is having *fun* learning.

A B C 20. The student should be rewarded in some way for the tasks successfully completed.

Answers can be found in the Appendix.

1.04 Reading Selection
So You Want to be a Tutor: Set Your Goals Now!

Purpose:
To provide goals towards which you should strive.

Directions:
Read and discuss the questions on the next page.

Here you are, maybe wondering what will be expected of you, who you will be working with, and maybe even, why you are here. Let me tell you something *special* about you. You are probably someone who likes to do well. You probably enjoy games, follow directions well, and generally get along well with your family, friends, and teachers. You like people and want to be liked too. You know how to be patient. You know how to make someone else feel special! That's what it is all about. The special characteristics that you have to offer a person are qualities that join and build *one* thing: *Caring.* Tutoring is caring.

There are six goals towards which the successful tutor will strive. *Caring is* the first. The most important characteristic of a tutor is your ability to care. Only by caring can you make someone else feel special and cared about. There is *no* other factor in the process of tutoring that will be more important or crucial to the success of tutoring than *caring*.

If you care, then you are already on your way to achieving your first goal.

Your second goal is the companion to caring. It is *Sharing*-to share is to give of yourself. It is to put your best side in front always and to give the best you have to offer. You must be willing to allow someone to share with you their thoughts, feelings, disappointments and successes. Most of all, you must be willing to *share you*.

The third goal is a real challenge, in fact it is *Challenge* itself. You probably face tutoring as a personal challenge for yourself. While it is good to consider tutoring a personal challenge, I am talking about the challenge which you must present to the students with whom you work. You must challenge your tutees to work very hard to achieve much and gain success in their endeavors. Truly that is a *challenge*.

As a tutor, you will assume the new roles of helper, friend, and *teacher.* These roles bring with them responsibilities, one of which is to *teach.* The fourth goal is to *teach. You* will notice that it is fourth for a reason. Teaching is important, but it cannot be done effectively until the other three goals have first been recognized and accepted as the base for your interaction. The teacher, or you as the tutor *must* care, share, and challenge first, only then can you begin to teach. View your responsibility to teach the assigned tasks as a very natural by-product of the first three goals. Once you have established that "caring" relationship with your tutee, begin to *teach.* And remember you can teach many more things than just what is written on the page in front of you.

A fifth goal is a bit more self-centered than the other four. Once you have achieved those four, you will deserve a little self-satisfaction. That is exactly what this goal is: *Satisfaction.* By striving for quality and success, you will also be realizing great satisfaction for yourself. You should look for it and then *enjoy* it.

Yes, you will take pleasure in helping others and in becoming a part of someone else's growth. Don't hesitate to seek actively the sixth goal: *Enjoyment.* Once you are familiar with your students, the material, your responsibilities, and self-discipline, the task of tutoring turns from duty to fun. You can *enjoy* being with someone who appreciates you and who wants to see you. You will become something for that person who no one else can-that person's personal private tutor. That means that you count as a special person. You will *matter* to someone else. *Enjoy* that.

Remember, success comes:

1. If you care,
2. If you will share,
3. If you will challenge,
4. If you will teach,
5. If you will satisfy,
6. If you will enjoy!

    If you will tutor!

... I have learned to be more patient and I have a tendency to be shy. However, by tutoring I have gained confidence and knowledge of other people. I feel that it is a stepping stone towards maturity. You are dealing with adult characteristics such as: caring, sharing, helping and teaching. I feel this class has something worthwhile and important to offer everyone.

Former Student Tutor

1.05 Reading Selection
Who is the Tutee?

Purpose:
To explain the term and concept "tutee."

Directions:
Read and discuss the following:

"As a result of my tutoring experiences, I have learned how to relate to people who I work with. This year I learned that no matter who you are, most everyone are alike in the things they do. Just because you happen to be a little better in one thing doesn't mean you are better in everything. If you are tutoring in English or something like that, your tutee could probably and most likely tutor you in one of the other school courses. We are not that much different...."

Former Student Tutor

The tutee or student receiving service is a fellow student who receives your service. The tutee is the one who can use help in some academic area. The tutee has strengths and weaknesses, as you, do, but the strengths may be in subjects other than your own. The tutee has talents that you may or may not possess. You may be a tutor in one subject and a tutee in another.

The tutee is someone who feels strongly about some things and less strongly about others. That is also like you. The tutee is a person with feelings who cares, shares, and wants to do well. Surprisingly, we all have feelings; we all want to care for and be cared about. The tutee will care about school work and want to experience success. You will have an opportunity, as a tutor, to be a part of that success. When you work with a student you must assume that the student *can* learn.

A student may not have been successful in a particular subject for several reasons. Often it is because there was not enough time spent to equip that student with adequate skills. Many times when one fails at something or is doing poorly, feelings of failure turn inward and the student begins to feel negatively. If you are enthusiastic, positive and reassuring, you can help reverse this attitude and provide an environment in which the student will want to learn and work hard. Once people have been convinced that they cannot do something, they believe it. It will be up to you to provide success for students and to help them recognize their potential.

The tutees to whom you are assigned will have an opportunity to get to know you, just as you will *make* the opportunity to get to know them.

Success for your tutees means success for you! Your tutee is a worthwhile person and deserves the right to achieve. Tutoring will be a learning experience for both of you.

Discussion Questions:
1. Describe who a tutee is.
2. What is your responsibility to the tutee?
3. How will you get to know the tutee? How will the tutee get to know you?

1.06 Activity
Success or Failure Questionnaire

Purpose:
To show that success/failure may not be determined in early life.

Directions:
Listed below are some examples of success or failure. Knowing *only* what is stated about the person, you must decide whether that person was *probably* a success or *probably* a failure in the chosen field by circling **S** for **Success** or **F** for **Failure**.

S F 1. Ran for political office seven times and was defeated each time.

S F 2. In writing, wrote a book that was rejected by every major publishing company in New York to which it was submitted, including Random House and Morrow.

S F 3. Wanted to be elected senator when he grew up. Was one of 35 to run for the president of his freshman class in college and was eliminated on the first ballot.

S F 4. Wanted to be a military leader or a great statesman. As a student failed three times in his exams to enter the British Military Academy.

S F 5. As a boy, had 24 brothers and sisters; his mother deserted the family when he was five; his father drank heavily; he lived in poverty; the children were put in foster homes; when he was seven he ran away eight times in one year; he was sent to reform school.

S F 6. In trying to solve a problem, tried 487 experiments all of which failed.

S F 7. Wanted to compose music, but became deaf.

S F 8. As a boy, flunked third grade; couldn't even take care of his own paper route.

S F 9. Wanted to be a performer; went to drama school in New York. After several months, the school wrote her mother that she had no acting ability at all. They said "take her back home."

S F 10. Wanted to get a British television series, *Till Death Do Us Part* on American prime time. He tried all networks for three years.

S F 11. Wanted to excel in science or engineering when he grew up. As a boy flunked first and fourth grades.

S F 12. Wanted to play an outstanding game as a quarterback. Completed only three of his first twelve passes; threw a total of thirty incomplete passes and one interception during the game.

S F 13. Wanted to be the outstanding baseball player in his league.

S F 14. Wanted to be a military leader, in military school he graduated 42 out of a class of 43—next to the last.

S F 15. Wanted to be an outstanding businessman. Wanted his own candy store. At 19, he tried to operate one, it failed. Went to New York and tried to manufacture candy. That failed too.

S F 16. Wanted to be a leader, ran for president of his senior class in high school and was defeated.

S F 17. Wanted to graduate from college and be a mathematician. Was expelled from school during his senior year because of bad grades and disciplinary problems. He never did graduate from high school.

S F 18. Wanted to play professional football, wasn't chosen through more than 200 draft choices. Finally, the Pittsburgh Steelers took him as their seventeenth pick. He didn't make the team. During the football training camp, they let him go.

S F 19. Wanted to sketch and cartoon. Applied for a job with a Kansas City newspaper. After looking at his work the editor said, "To be frank with you, it's easy to see from these sketches that you have no talent."

S F 20. In sports, struck out 1,330 times in baseball.

S F 21. Wanted to be governor of his state. Ran for governor and lost.

The answers to each item are in the Appendix.

Tutoring: Learning by Helping

1.07 Reading Selection

Being Real

Purpose:

To provide an example that demonstrates what is meant by "being real" and cared about.

Directions:

Read and discuss the following:

The Velveteen Rabbit

"What is *real?* asked the Rabbit one day, when they were lying side by side near the nursery fender, before Nana came to tidy the room. "Does it mean having things that buzz inside you and a stick-out handle?"

"Real isn't how you are made," said the Skin Horse. "It's a thing that happens to you. When a child loves you for a long, long time, not just to play with, but *really* loves you, then you become Real."

"Does it hurt?" asked the Rabbit.

"Sometimes," said the Skin Horse, for he was always truthful. "When you are Real you don't mind being hurt."

"Does it happen all at once, like being wound up," he asked, "or bit by bit ? "

"It doesn't happen all at once," said the Skin Horse. "You become. It takes a long time. That's why it doesn't often happen to people who break easily, or have sharp edges, or who have to be carefully kept. Generally, by the time you are Real, most of your hair has been loved off, and your eyes drop out and you get loose in the joints and very shabby. But these things don't matter at all, because once you are Real you can't be ugly, except to people who don't understand."

"I suppose you are Real?" said the Rabbit. And then he wished he had not said it, for he thought the Skin Horse might be sensitive, but the Skin Horse only smiled.

"The Boy's Uncle made me Real," he said. "That was a great many years ago; but once you are Real you can't become unreal again. It lasts for always."

Discussion/Questions:

1. Discuss how long it takes to be loved or cared about?
2. What does it take to show real care or love?
3. How might a tutor put to practice the message of "Being Real?"

Elizabeth Sabrinsky Foster, Ed.D.

Chapter 1 — Orientation to Tutoring

1.08 Follow-up Exercise
Success and Being Real

Purpose:

To provide an opportunity to relate Being Real to success in tutoring.

Directions:

You have recently completed the *Success/Failure Questionnaire* and read a portion of *The Velveteen Rabbit In* Reading Selection 1.07. Let's consider how these two items relate to your study of tutoring.

Success:

We should set goals for ourselves and we do. We shouldn't be afraid to have high standards and have high expectations for ourselves. Sometimes we don't always reach every goal, in fact we probably *can't* reach every goal. Does that mean we should stop trying when we meet our first disappointment? No, definitely not.

Failure:

Tutoring may present you with some disappointments. An example of disappointment may be that your students do not progress as quickly or as successfully as you would like, but that is part of trial and error, part of the challenge that life provides us as we find windows to open when doors close.

The people you read about in the *Success/Failure Questionnaire* became very famous in some area of their lives, *but* they all experienced a type of failure during the climb. These are the people that didn't give up and say: "Well, I can't do it if I'm not on top the first time." These are the people that had stamina. They learned from disappointment and from experience. They learned to *be real* during their climb to success.

You know *The Velveteen Rabbit* is only a fairy tale, but just as the Skin Horse in *The Velveteen Rabbit* wanted to become real, you will be "real" too—before the year is over.

Discussion Questions:

1. Find the parts of the selection from *Being Real* that you could use to answer a fellow student who asked: "How will you know when you're real as a tutor?"
2. How will you know if you're successful in tutoring?

1.09 Activity
The Animal School

Purpose:

To illustrate differences in people and the uniqueness of each individual.

Directions:

Read the following in preparation for activity 1.10.

The Administration of the School Curriculum with References to Individual Differences

by

Dr. George H. Reavis

Assistant Superintendent

Cincinnati Public Schools, 1939-1948

Once upon a time, the animals decided they must do something heroic to meet the problems of "a new world." So they organized a school.

They adopted an activity curriculum consisting of running, climbing, swimming, and flying. To make it easier to administer the curriculum all the animals took all the subjects.

The duck was excellent in swimming, in fact better than his instructor; but he made only passing grades in flying and was very poor in running. Since he was slow in running, he had to stay after school and also drop swimming in order to practice running. This was kept up until his web feet were badly worn and he was only average in swimming. But average was acceptable in school so nobody worried about that except the duck.

The rabbit started at the top of the class in running, but had a nervous breakdown because of so much make-up work in swimming.

The squirrel was excellent in climbing until he developed frustration in the flying class when his teacher made him start from the ground instead of from the tree top down. He also developed a "Charlie horse" from over-exertion and then got C in climbing and D in running

The eagle was a problem child and was disciplined severely. In the climbing class he beat all the others to the top of the tree, but insisted on using his own way to get there.

At the end of the year, an abnormal eel that could swim exceedingly well, and also ran, climb and fly a little, had the highest average and was valedictorian.

The prairie dogs stayed out of school and fought the tax levy because the administration would not add digging and burrowing to the curriculum. They apprenticed their children to a badger and later joined the groundhogs and gophers to start a successful private school.

Materials:

1. Copy of Reading, *The Animal School*
2. *Tutor School Report Card* (hand out)
3. One box of small paper clips
4. One box of large paper clips
5. Magic markers or crayons
6. Masking tape
7. Blank paper for folding and drawing
8. A box of envelopes or rubber bands
9. Bullseye on a poster

Directions:

1. Read *The Animal School*. This allows you to discuss the differences and sameness in how people might be educated in public systems much like the animals.
2. If you are in a class of *25:*
   a. Five volunteers are selected; the remaining students are divided into four groups.
   b. Each volunteer will serve as the instructor for *one* of the tutor classes: Airplane Folding and Flying, Paper Clip Throwing, Rubber Bands, Bozo Art, and Snowflake Design. (Other classes may be listed as alternates or options as the leader chooses.)
   c. The job of instructor for each of the "classes" is explained to the volunteers. Descriptions follow at the end of these directions.
   d. Each tutor/instructor takes an assigned place and the groups assemble around them.
   e. Each class lasts five minutes.
   f. At the end of five minutes, the groups rotate to another class. The instructors stay put and teach again for four for five minutes.
   g. At the end of the each five-minute class period, the instructor gives each student a letter grade to be recorded on the *Tutor School Report Card*.
   h. The rotation occurs until all of the students have attended all of the classes.
   i. At the end of the classes, the instructors give a report on their students. Time should also be allowed for the students to report on the teachers and the classes. Their reactions and feelings should be included.
   j. Discuss what was learned through this activity. Be sure to process all components.
3. If you are in a class of 8-16:
   a. Instead of dividing the class into four or five, make only two groups. Ask for volunteers to be instructors. However, only two classes should operate at a time.
   b. The rotation occurs until all four or five classes have been taught.

Directions for Classes:

All instructors should give information to their students. They should model the behavior they want and explain how they will be grading. Practice time should be provided. A bell should ring after four minutes to alert the instructors that there is one minute left.

1. The *Bozo Art* class is designed for students to be involved in a creative activity. The students are to draw and color a picture of a Bozo clown. They may be graded on uniqueness, creativity, or their ability to replicate a clown drawn by the Bozo Art instructor. That decision is left to the instructor. The final artwork may be displayed.
2. *Paper Clip Throwing* is an activity of dexterity. The instructor should place a line of masking tape at the point where the participants stand. A second line of tape is placed approximately three feet away. This is the line onto which the paper clips should be tossed. The students can be graded according to the number of successful tries or the closeness of the paper clips to the line.
3. The *Rubber Band* class provides an opportunity for hand-eye coordination. A bullseye should be drawn on a poster. This should then be placed on the wall for the students to shoot at. The students can be directed to stand at a certain point. They should be graded according to how close they shoot or how many times they hit the bullseye.
4. *Snowflake Design* is an art class that allow students to demonstrate creativity. Snowflakes are made by either tearing pieces from the paper or using scissors to cut. Grades are determined by the criteria set by the instructor.

5. *Airplane Folding and Flying* is a class that allow expression of design and flights. The students can be shown a design pattern to copy or be allowed to make their own. Their flights are part of the grade. They may be graded on the number of successful flights or the distance or height or a creative endeavor.

Other classes that can be substituted: Domino Stacking, Speed Magazine Folding, Blowing Bubbles or Bubble Gum Race, Ping Pong Floor Race, and Card Stacking.

Discussion:

1. Discuss teaching characteristics which seem to make more successful classes..
2. Discuss student performance, grades, and attitudes and how they related to teaching and classes..
3. Relate this experience to tutoring. What do we need to remember?
4. How alike and different were the students?
5. How did it feel to try and perform well in front of your peers?

Tutor School Report Card

Student_____ Date_____

	Grade	Teacher Initials
Bozo Art Class	_____	_____
Paper Clip Throwing	_____	_____
Rubber Bands	_____	_____
Snowflake Design	_____	_____
Airplane Flying	_____	_____

1.10 Activity
Circle Gram

Purpose:

To determine how people's perceptions of each other affect interaction.

Directions:

1. Look at the *Circle Gram* on the following page. You will see a number of different interest areas. Pick the three areas that interest you the most. List them below:

   Your Interests			Checkmarks
   1. _____		_____
   2. _____		_____
   3. _____		_____

2. Look at each member in your class group. Write each person's name in each interest category on the *Circle Gram* in which you think that person might have an interest or skill. A particular student's name may appear in several categories.

3. After everyone has filled out their *Circle Grams*, share your *Circle Grams* with the class. Place a checkmark on the line after your top three interests every time your name is called out indicating someone else sees you as having that interest.

4. If you hear your name called out in a category other than your top three interests, place the check mark on your *Circle Gram* below the name of the category.

Discussion Questions:

1. What does this activity tell you about how other people see you and what they think you like?
2. What does this activity tell you about how you see other people and the things you think they like?
3. How can you use this information in your tutoring experience?

Circle Gram

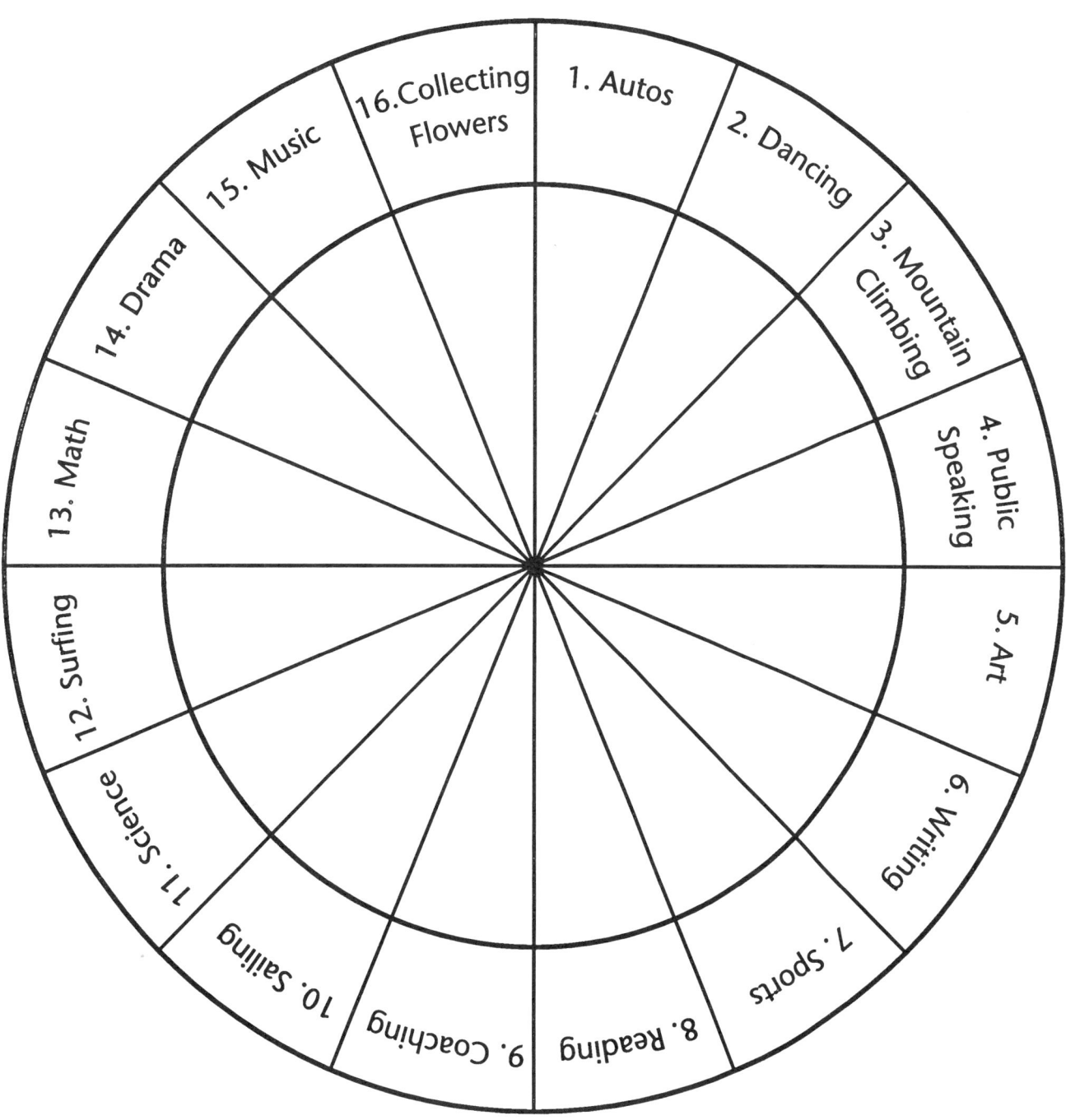

1.11 Reading Selection

Motivation and Needs: Useful Theories

Purpose:
To provide information on the basic needs of each individual as applied to tutoring.

Directions:

Read and discuss the following:

Understanding interactions between people in dyads or groups begins with understanding the individual and recognizing personal needs. People are highly motivated to satisfy their own needs. If we cannot satisfy our needs, then the motive for doing so will become stronger and stronger until some resolution is found.

An example of this might be: Imagine someone staying awake for three days and nights in a row. A strong need to sleep would surely develop. The motivating factor would be fatigue or tiredness. Without sleep there would be very little productive work, in fact, the individual would probably think of nothing but sleep.

Personality is affected by physiological or biological needs, particularly when the needs are not met. An ordinarily calm person who experiences body coldness because of the low temperature in a room may become very irritable until able to meet the need for warmth. The biological or basic physiological needs of each must be met for the personality to function satisfactorily.

When people function or interact in dyads or groups, their psychological needs must also be met before they can be positive functioning members of the group. Insight into why people behave as they do can be gained by exploring the developmental needs of humans. This information can be valuable in analyzing the best way to interact with people. In tutoring, the recognition of individual needs is crucial to the success of the tutoring environment and relationship. The tutor must understand that every individual has both basic and very sophisticated needs. The tutor must understand that to prevent another person from satisfaction of needs will only create a greater motivation to satisfy any probable frustration which might impede the progress of the tutoring work. The tutor who understands can better predict the behavior of the tutees as well as facilitate a warm learning environment.

A well known psychologist, Abraham Maslow, developed a theory regarding human needs and motivation that is useful in understanding the motivating factors that affect behavior and personality.

Basic to Maslow's theory is a classification system of human needs. He presents a hierarchy of five categories of need in the order of importance.

1. **Physiological needs** are directly related to survival and self preservation. Primary survival needs include such things as the need for oxygen, food, water, rest, exercise, excretion, and avoidance of bodily harm. Maslow believed these needs are so important that a person can do or think of little else until they are satisfactorily met. However, their importance diminishes as they become satisfied or are in a state of equilibrium, and the next category of needs on the hierarchy comes into play.

2. **Safety needs** are related to psychological safety or security and reflect a desire to be safe from personal violence or harm, as well as to avoid the unpredictable.

3. **Love needs** are related to a desire for a sense of belonging and acceptance. Satisfaction involves both opportunities for giving and receiving.

4. **Esteem needs** go beyond love needs into a more active desire for recognition and self-esteem. Maslow classified these into two sub-categories: (l) the desire for strength or achievement and (2) the desire for recognition, importance and appreciation. Satisfaction leads to self-confidence.

5. **Self-actualization needs** come into prominence once all the lower needs are met to a satisfactory degree. These include the need for a person to maximize potential; to reach the peak of unique abilities and talents. Creativity, curiosity, ambition, and independence are all related to self-actualization. Unlike the house pet that only strives to be well fed, warm and cuddled, the human animal strives for much more that often takes forms of expression through creative or competitive efforts in the arts, sciences, athletics, or religious life.

Maslow's Hierarchy of Needs

<u>Highest Level</u>

5
Self-Actualization Needs
Self-fulfillment
Self-growth
Uniqueness

4
Esteem Needs
Self-respect
Recognition
Self-esteem
Status
Prestige
Attention

3
Love Needs
Acceptance
Love
Friendship
Understanding

2
Safety Needs
Structure
Order
Security
Protection
Freedom from fear

1
Physiological Needs

<u>Lowest Level</u>

Food
Water
Air
Warmth

As lower level needs are met, higher levels come into play.

Discussion Questions:

1. What would the reaction be of one of your tutees if the need for food or warmth had not been met?
2. How does safety play a factor for tutees and their ability to concentrate?
3. What safety factors might concern your tutee?
4. What can you do to promote meeting the higher levels of need as classified by Maslow?

1.12 Activity
Self-Effectiveness Chart

Purpose:
To determine if your self-concept is basically negative or positive.

Directions:
On a scale of 1-10, circle the number as you see yourself for each item listed. When you have completed that, connect each circle with a line to form a graph. You may choose to do this again at the completion of the tutoring experience to determine if you have increased your own self-effectiveness. Complete follow-up exercise 1.13.

Self-Effectiveness Chart

1 2 3 4 5 6 7 8 9 10   1. Energy level.
1 2 3 4 5 6 7 8 9 10   2. Enthusiasm.
1 2 3 4 5 6 7 8 9 10   3. Communication skills.
1 2 3 4 5 6 7 8 9 10   4. Understanding of people.
1 2 3 4 5 6 7 8 9 10   5. Planning ability.
1 2 3 4 5 6 7 8 9 10   6. Use of creativity.
1 2 3 4 5 6 7 8 9 10   7. Persuasiveness.
1 2 3 4 5 6 7 8 9 10   8. Executive (carry out/carry through).
1 2 3 4 5 6 7 8 9 10   9. Understanding of self.
1 2 3 4 5 6 7 8 9 10 10. Ambition.
1 2 3 4 5 6 7 8 9 10 11. Concern for others.
1 2 3 4 5 6 7 8 9 10 12. Self-motivation.
1 2 3 4 5 6 7 8 9 10 13. Time management skills.
1 2 3 4 5 6 7 8 9 10 14. Aspiration for excellence.
1 2 3 4 5 6 7 8 9 10 15. Self-discipline.
1 2 3 4 5 6 7 8 9 10 16. Problem-solving ability.
1 2 3 4 5 6 7 8 9 10 17. Self confidence.
1 2 3 4 5 6 7 8 9 10 18. Interest in school.
1 2 3 4 5 6 7 8 9 10 19. Emotional control.
1 2 3 4 5 6 7 8 9 10 20. Speaking ability before others.
1 2 3 4 5 6 7 8 9 10 21. Positive attitudes.
1 2 3 4 5 6 7 8 9 10 22. Ability to work with others.

1.13 Follow-up Exercise
Self-Effectiveness Analysis

Purpose:

To provide feedback on the Self-Effectiveness Chart.

Directions:

You have just completed the *Self-Effectiveness Chart*. The items listed are those characteristics most often accepted as being necessary characteristics to success in any job you attempt.

Many people limit their growth by not seeing themselves realistically. In fact, many people underestimate their own abilities—weaknesses seem to dominate the strengths.

This chart is an opportunity for you to evaluate "how you see yourself." Look at it and determine if this represents a positive or negative self-image.

Whenever you look at yourself closely, keep in mind that what you are seeing is a picture of that moment. It is as if someone took a picture of you today, developed the negative of the picture, but took the negative out too soon and the picture was underdeveloped. Take another picture tomorrow-the same process. This time the negative may be more developed, at least it will be slightly different. Each of us is an underdeveloped picture in the process of development.

The characteristics listed can be acquired and developed more fully as you become more aware of them. The attitude you bring to each "photo" session determines your self-image.

Now look again at your chart. The space to the left-hand side of your line represents what you are today. The space on the right-hand side represents what you can be-what potential lies ahead-the part of you that is still underdeveloped. Maybe throughout this year you will put a bit more developer solution on these characteristics so that the potential that lies ahead will truly start to develop.

Interaction:

Divide into dyads and discuss the characteristics and how they related to success in school, work, and tutoring. Ask each partner to review the other's graph; ask questions about the interest by the partner to develop and identify at least two characteristics that will be developed through some goal-setting process.

1.14 Activity
It's Tough Being Human

Purpose:

To determine specific strengths and weaknesses that relate to tutoring.

Directions:

List below those activities with which you have difficulty and those things with which you have no difficulty. (Examples: sports, academics, making friends, singing, and so forth) Be sure these are specific things you do.

Tough Ones	Easy Ones

List below who or what could help you with the items listed in the "Tough Ones" category.

Discussion Questions:

1. How many "tough ones" were listed?
2. Did your people list include a variety of people?
3. What does this activity tell us about people and our relationship to tutoring?

1.15 Follow-up Exercise
It's Tough Being Human—Look Again

Purpose:

To provide feedback on the previous activity and to focus on eliminating a weakness.

Directions:

How you see yourself is a crucial element to your ability to achieve success. Your attitude about yourself is seen in everything you say and do. No matter what the task, how well you accomplish it is affected by how you feel about yourself at the appointed time of the task. How well you communicate with others is either negatively or positively influenced by how you are feeling about yourself.

If when you listed your tough and easy ones, you listed more tough ones than easy ones, at that moment, your self-image may have been more negative than positive. Too many negative days can be habit-forming. Too much energy used for negative activities produces bad experiences and sours your attitudes toward you by yourself and others.

Look again at your list and see if you have overlooked some of your positive strengths. Are there some talents, special abilities or gifts that you have, that you left out?

Brainstorm for a moment on those things we take for granted that you might add to your list.

Remember that you can always become a stronger person. Look at your lists. Choose *one* that you will concentrate upon improving for the next week.

List a tough one _____

_____

Now list the steps you will follow to try and strengthen a difficult area:

1. _____
2. _____
3. _____
4. _____

In one week, return to this page and evaluate how many steps you followed and try to determine your effectiveness in what you identified. Remember: Identifying a weakness is a strength. Eliminating a weakness is a credit to you.

Why do this?

As Socrates said, "Know thyself." You must understand yourself before you begin to know and understand others.

1.16 Reading and Activity
What is This Thing Called Confidentiality?

Purpose:

To understand what it means to keep something confidential.

Directions:

Read the following and apply it everyday in your activities as a tutor.

"Confidentiality" is the keeping of private information private. Very simply that means: Don't repeat what you talk about in tutoring to another individual. Do not discuss tutoring sessions with any other person other than the teacher or tutee. Treat each person with whom you deal as you would hope others would treat you. It is your obligation to respect the right of privacy of your tutees. Gain the right of trust.

Consider the following points regarding confidentiality:

1. Tutors must act in an ethical manner and adhere to a high standard of conduct.
2. Tutors must mind their own business and not interfere with that of the other tutors or students during sessions.
3. Tutors must not talk about any student or teacher or tutoring situation outside of the training area.
4. Telling just one person, even your best friend, about some confidential matter, breaks the ethical code of confidence.
5. Remember, it takes weeks and months to build the trust of another person, but only a minute to destroy it.

Exceptions:

They only exceptions to the confidentiality rule are:

A. If someone is going to hurt himself or herself.

B. If someone else is going to be hurt.

These situations need to be reported to your coordinator/trainer.

Elizabeth Sabrinsky Foster, Ed.D.

Chapter 2
Developing Helping Relationships in Tutoring

Chapter Concepts:
1. You can develop skills that will enable you to serve in helping roles.
2. By understanding personal needs, you can better meet other's needs.
3. You must avoid stereotyping others to be an effective helper.

Chapter Objectives:
1. To help you to identify your personal needs.
2. To learn how to develop positive rapport with each tutee.

Chapter Description:
This chapter explains the components of helping relationships, and explores ways to establish, maintain and nurture those relationships. It is important to know about your own needs before you attempt to help others meet theirs. You will learn about the different kinds of roles people can play in helping others and to recognize the characteristics which are most successful in developing helping relationships.

Chapter Vocabulary:
elements, confidence, impressions, stereotype

Contents

2.01	Acceptance	Reading Selection	20
2.02	Developing a Helping Relationship	Activity	21
2.03	Helping Relationship Scale	Activity	22
2.04	Lincoln Logs Can Help	Activity	22
2.05	Detecting Stereotypes	Activity	24

2.01 Reading Selection

Acceptance

Purpose:

To help form an "accepting" attitude.

Directions:

Read and discuss the following:

I accept you.

I approve of you.

I am satisfied with who you are today-not merely with who you may be tomorrow.

You have a right to your uniqueness. I do not need to change you.

There is a constant quality within you that I like-even when it lies hidden beneath some of your actions.

You see... I like you, but not everything you do or say.

I can separate your actions from you, because I realize that you don't always do what you want to do-that you are not always aware and in control-that you are struggling to be happy in the best way you know-just as I am.

So, you can fall on your face, change your mind, get into trouble-and I will not laugh or condemn you.

I will not call you names like "failure" or "troublemaker" or "hypocrite." I will not pin labels on you like "dumb" or "lazy" or bad."

Instead of making judgments about who you are, I will concentrate on how I feel about your actions.

I will not call you "bad" but I will tell you if I feel "bad" about what you have done.

In this way, you can know my limits and realize that you are lovable even though some of your actions are not.

But I must warn you: The more you hurt me, the harder it is for me to accept you.

I cannot be forever patient and tolerant....

I am human and need acceptance too.

Discussion Questions:

1. What does this poem say about accepting people?
2. Does the poet suggest their are limits to acceptance or limits to tolerance?
3. How does the poet separate behaviors or actions from feelings about the person?
4. Relate the message expressed to the tutoring situation.

2.02 Activity

Developing a Helping Relationship

Purpose:

To provide information on the elements of a "helping relationship."

Directions:

Read the following and complete the *Helping Relationship Rating Scale*.

Developing the skills that will enable you to "help" someone else is an important component of your training. A "helping relationship" is a bit different from other relationships that you may make. It sounds simple enough. We know that "helping" means to give assistance. We also know that "relationship" means interaction of two or more people from which a bond is formed. The issue at hand is: What kind of bond is formed? It will be up to you to set the guidelines for your relationship and create a trusting environment in which it can grow.

Let's look at the parts of a "helping relationship."

1. Purpose
2. Caring
3. Trust
4. Confidence
5. Understanding
6. Communication

You will find some or all of those elements existing in relationships based on friendship, love, professionalism or family ties. The major differences in those relationships and the "helping relationship" is for "helping" to occur there is an established purpose and goal. To be successful in reaching the goal, all six elements must be present during the developing helping relationship. As the "helping relationship" grows, other characteristics or types of relationships may develop simultaneously. For example, people who enter into "helping relationships" may also enter into friendship. That is fine and often times this does happen. But keep in mind, our initial goal is to form a helping relationship and to assist another student to improve academic performance in one or more courses.

Let's look more closely at the six elements and how each plays a part in the successful and healthy "helping relationship."

1. What is purpose?

Purpose is the reason for establishing the relationship. In the case of tutoring, the purpose is improvement of academic ability. Not only should you have an established purpose, but you should have a thorough understanding of the short and long range goals associated with the purpose.

2. What is caring?

Caring is the demonstration on the part of the tutor of a caring attitude. You must be able to show that this person does matter to you and that you care about this person's progress. Let others know how important they are.

3. What is trust?

Trust is the feeling you give other persons when they know they can share personal feelings, successes and failures. You can be counted upon to keep information to yourself that may be personal. You allow someone else to be honest. Trust is a building block for all relationships that are successful and essential to relationships that survive time.

4. What is confidence?

Confidence is knowing that you can be depended upon and that you will follow through. It is knowing that you have the information or will get it for the tasks involved in the relationship. Be honest with yourself and the receiving person in the relationship.

5. What is understanding?

Understanding is your ability to be patient, empathic and sincere in dealing with the task and the person whom you are helping. You must be able to put yourself in the other person's shoes and look through that person's eyes. When you can do that your depth of understanding will indeed be developed.

6. What is communication?

Communication is the tool we all use to express our thoughts and feelings. We can express ourselves through verbal as well as non-verbal means. Communication skills in a helping relationship should be refined to assure that sender and receiver in the relationship have a two-way communication flow.

All six of the listed elements must be present to support and nurture helping relationships. You have the responsibility to continuously refine each component of the helping relationship as you tutor through the year.

To help you determine how you presently see yourself in relation to the six components of a helping relationship, complete the *Helping Relationship Rating Scale*. This will be a guide for you in looking at elements you will need to strengthen.

2.03 Activity
Helping Relationship Rating Scale

Directions:

By each element, evaluate your skill level on a 5-point scale with **1** = low and **5** = high.

1 2 3 4 5   1. **Purpose:** Your understanding of the goals of tutoring.

1 2 3 4 5   2. **Caring:** Your ability to demonstrate a caring attitude.

1 2 3 4 5   3. **Trust:** Your ability to create a feeling of honesty and openness.

1 2 3 4 5   4. **Confidence:** Your ability to develop an attitude in others that shows you are dependable and knowledgeable.

1 2 3 4 5   5. **Understanding:** Your willingness to look at issues and problems through the eyes of someone else.

1 2 3 4 5   6. **Communication:** Your skill at being an "effective" communicator.

Process:

You may wish to discuss how you see yourself now. Complete this scale after training to determine your readiness to serve as a helper.

2.04 Activity
Lincoln Logs Can Help

Purpose:

To establish a criteria for the "helping" characteristics.

Directions:

After observing a builder and helper construct a house of Lincoln Logs in *three minutes,* rate the house as follows. (Roles for builders and helpers can be found in the Appendix.)

Rate each house Excellent (4), Good (3), Fair (2), and Poor (1) on each of the criteria listed on the House Rating Scale on the next page.

After each house has been completed with the volunteer builder and helper, the audience tallies the score for each house, identifying the characteristics of each helper and how those characteristics helped to accomplish the task. In a discussion, determine which pair was the most able to work together and what they accomplished. What interfered with the other pairs?

Process:

1. Determine the most effective helping characteristics.
2. How do you think helping can best be achieved?

House Rating Scale

	House 1	House 2	House 3	House 4	House 5
Stability					
Height					
Attractiveness					
Windows and Doors					
Completion					
Landscaping					
Creativeness					
Roofline-Proportion					
House Score:					

Identify the Helpers

	Builder Names	Helper Names	Kind of Helper
1			
2			
3			
4			
5			

Tutoring: Learning by Helping

2.05 Activity

Detecting Stereotypes

Purpose:
To determine what assumptions you will make based on a small amount of information.

Directions:
Below are descriptions of eight different people. From the bit of information given, circle the number which best indicates your perception of that sort of person. Each of the ten are based on a scale of 1-5.

1. Miss Winthrop, a teacher at Miller Junior High School, has taught there for ten years. She is 5'2" and loves teaching math classes. She probably is:

Intelligent	1	2	3	4	5	Stupid
Easygoing	1	2	3	4	5	Hot-tempered
Lenient	1	2	3	4	5	Strict
Conservative	1	2	3	4	5	Liberal
Ambitious	1	2	3	4	5	Lazy

2. Mr. Smith, 45 years old, is the local state highway patrolman. He is married, has three children and two cats. He probably is:

Intelligent	1	2	3	4	5	Stupid
Easygoing	1	2	3	4	5	Hot-tempered
Lenient	1	2	3	4	5	Strict
Conservative	1	2	3	4	5	Liberal
Ambitious	1	2	3	4	5	Lazy

3. Bill is a 16-year-old high school junior in a city school. He works as a lifeguard every summer, dates every weekend and enjoys cars. He probably is:

Intelligent	1	2	3	4	5	Stupid
Easygoing	1	2	3	4	5	Hot-tempered
Friendly	1	2	3	4	5	Unfriendly
Conservative	1	2	3	4	5	Liberal
Ambitious	1	2	3	4	5	Lazy

4. Harry works as a garbage collector. He is married and has one child. He probably is:

Intelligent	1	2	3	4	5	Stupid
Easygoing	1	2	3	4	5	Hot-tempered
Friendly	1	2	3	4	5	Unfriendly
Attractive	1	2	3	4	5	Unattractive
Ambitious	1	2	3	4	5	Lazy

5. Caroline is a senior at the University of North Carolina. She is 5'2" and loves English classes. She probably is:

Intelligent	1	2	3	4	5	Stupid
Easygoing	1	2	3	4	5	Hot-tempered
Lenient	1	2	3	4	5	Strict
Conservative	1	2	3	4	5	Liberal
Attractive	1	2	3	4	5	Unattractive

6. Mr. Brown, 45 years old, is the town street cleaner. He is married, has three children and two cats. He probably is

Intelligent	1	2	3	4	5	Stupid
Easygoing	1	2	3	4	5	Hot-tempered
Lenient	1	2	3	4	5	Strict
Conservative	1	2	3	4	5	Liberal
Ambitious	1	2	3	4	5	Lazy

7. William is a 26-year-old high school teacher. He works as a lifeguard every summer, dates every weekend and enjoys cars. He probably is:

Intelligent	1	2	3	4	5	Stupid
Easygoing	1	2	3	4	5	Hot-tempered
Friendly	1	2	3	4	5	Unfriendly
Conservative	1	2	3	4	5	Liberal
Attractive	1	2	3	4	5	Unattractive

8. Robert works as a tax accountant. He is married and has one child. He probably is:

Intelligent	1	2	3	4	5	Stupid
Easygoing	1	2	3	4	5	Hot-tempered
Friendly	1	2	3	4	5	Unfriendly
Ambitious	1	2	3	4	5	Lazy
Attractive	1	2	3	4	5	Unattractive

Processing:

To begin discussion, define the word "stereotype." List on the board some common physical stereotypes such as: wearing glasses means you are smart. List on the board some common "work related" stereotypes such as: Blue collar jobs involve dirty work. Continue to list as many stereotypes as possible.

Look through the descriptions and circle any parts of the descriptions which represent a stereotype. Note that in this list there are matching descriptions and only one part has been changed. Often only the male or female role is changed. What are the implications of the decisions made by the group? How does this apply to tutoring? Compare the group answers.

Chapter 3
Communication Skills

Chapter Concepts:

1. The more you know about the process of communication, the better able you are able to communicate.
2. The more tutors practice "attending" skills, the more effective they are in tutoring.

Chapter Objectives:

To help you to develop the listening, observing, speaking, non-verbal and feedback skills that are necessary to be an effective tutor.

Chapter Description:

This chapter explains the necessary components of effective communication. It provides exercises for you to develop skills that will help you to become an effective communicator. The lessons learned in this chapter will be useful in tutoring as well as in all aspects of your daily life.

Chapter Vocabulary:

interpersonal communication, feedback, sender, receiver, body language, verbal and nonverbal, gestures, attending behavior, barrier, affective, cognitive

Contents

3.01	Communication Pre-Test	Activity	27
3.02	Elements of Communication	Reading Selection	28
3.03	Dominoes for Feedback	Activity	29
3.04	What is Listening?	Activity	30
3.05	Unfocused Listening	Reading Selection	31
3.06	Levels of Listening	Reading Selection	32
3.07	Pass the Rumor	Activity	33
3.08	Biography for Non-listeners	Activity	33
3.09	The Happy Hooker	Activity	34
3.10	Act Like a Listener	Reading Selection	34
3.11	Eye to Eye Contact	Reading Selection	35
3.12	Do You Know What Your Voice Reveals?	Reading Selection	36
3.13	Communication of Thoughts and Feelings	Reading Selection	37
3.14	Roadblocks to Communication	Activity	38
3.15	Using the Feeling Side: Appropriate Responses	Activity	40
3.16	Select the "Effective" Feeling Response	Skills Practice	42
3.17	Tutoring Simulation: Tape the Tutor	Activity	44

Chapter 3 — Communication Skills

3.01 Activity
Communication Pre-Test

Purpose:
To determine your present level of understanding regarding communication.

Directions:
Test your understanding of what communication is by taking the following pre-test. Circle T for True or F for False as it applies to each statement. The activities that follow will enlighten you concerning the concepts you do not understanding.

T F 1. One person is sufficient for communication.

T F 2. In communication with another person, the sender hopes that the receiver will change in some way.

T F 3. Communication is a series of messages.

T F 4. A person's attitude can affect the ability to communicate.

T F 5. Your voice can reveal how you feel.

T F 6. Communication could be as simple as reading this book.

T F 7. If you express only what other people think, communication is not open.

T F 8. Body language deals only with the way you walk and sit.

T F 9. Clarity in communication is a vital tool to effective communication.

T F 10. Feedback is the process of the sender giving the message.

T F 11. Feedback is used to demonstrate truth in statements.

T F 12. Eyes can be a vital tool in effective communication.

T F 13. Certain verbal responses may be inappropriate for the situation.

T F 14. Communication in groups is as important as in interpersonal communication .

T F 15. Without a receiver, there can be no communication.

T F 16. Nonverbal communication deals with silent messages.

T F 17. Communication skills will limit your growth as a student or tutor.

3.02 Reading Selection

Elements of Communication

Purpose:

To provide information on elements and types of communication.

Directions:

Read and discuss the following:

Communication is a means of developing relationships. It allows you to send messages, to interpret feelings and to express opinions. The human ability to communicate is unique and provides us with unique opportunities. As a tutor you will also have unique opportunities. Those opportunities bring with them responsibilities. The better able you are to communicate with those around you, the better able you will be to carry out your responsibility as a tutor. In addition to becoming a better tutor, you'll find that developing communication skills will increase the likelihood of your being a better student, friend, brother/sister, club member, and so forth. Communication skills are valuable for all aspects of your life.

In tutoring you will need to be able to relate to another person on at least two levels: academic and personal. For you to do this you must first know basic elements of communication. Therefore, we will read, study and practice activities related to the following:

1. Basic elements of communication
2. Basic types of communication
3. Effective methods of communication

What are the basic elements of communication?

There are four basic elements of communication. All four elements should be present for complete and effective communication to take place.

A. **Sender:** The sender is the person who wishes to communicate a thought, feeling, or expression.

B. **Receiver:** The receiver is the one for whom the thought, feeling or expression is intended.

C. **Message:** The message is the thought, feeling, opinion, or expression that is shared.

D. **Feedback:** Feedback is the opportunity for each person to make sure the listener understands the messages. Nylen, et. al (1967) defined feedback as communication which gives back to another individual information about how one has affected us and how one stands with us in relation to one's goals or intentions. This information can be either positive or negative.

What types of communication are there?

There are two major types of communication:

A. **Nonverbal:** Nonverbal communication is that which involves silent forms of communication. It includes all those things that you can do to communicate without speaking. You might use a written form or you might use your body. For example, you might make a gesture with your hand to indicate you would like a person to move. You might nod your head in a response to a question, indicating your answer. Any time you use your body consciously or unconsciously to send a message without speaking, you are using "body language."

Body language is the major form of nonverbal communication. It lets the receiver of the information know how you feel by the way your body responds. Body language involves the way you sit, the way you move, the direction your eyes dart and everything that involves responses.

B. **Verbal:** Verbal communication is what we use most of the time to consciously send messages in the form of speech.

What is necessary for effective communication to take place?

A. The four elements of communication
B. Positive nonverbal language
C. Well developed "attending skills"

Definitions:

Attending is a term often associated with communication in helping relationships. 'Attending" is paying particular attention to the person with whom you are communicating.

Positive attending behavior implies that the tutors will focus all attention and interest on the tutee.

Attending behaviors of the sender:

1. Maintain eye-to-eye contact.
2. Demonstrate positive body language.
3. Provide opportunity for feedback.
4. Give wait time.
5. Focus on the receiver.

Attending behaviors of the receiver:

Chapter 3 — Communication Skills

1. Maintain eye-to-eye contact.
2. Demonstrate positive body language.
3. Respond when appropriate
4. Give wait time
5. Focus on the sender.
6. Be an *Active Listener.*

It might be helpful if you think of attending skills as those that help you *FOCUS*. Describing what each letter in *FOCUS* means will help insure that you will both understand it and do it!

F = Full attention
O = Open
C = Center yourself
U = Use eyes and ear
S = Smile and relax

If you will use the *FOCUS* approach, you will be on your way to a life of "attending."

It is necessary to remember that the responsibilities of the listener are just as important as those of the speaker. Active listening means remaining silent when the other person is talking about a concern. The listener periodically reflects back to the speaker in a few words an understanding of the speaker's words and feelings. Active listening creates a climate of trust and acceptance.

As a tutor you will have the opportunity and challenge to communicate many things. Sharing information is just one of the many things you will communicate. You will be able to communicate positive attitudes about learning. You will be able to communicate the need for responsible behavior. You will be able to communicate that you care.

That's a lot to communicate!

Practice:

1. Volunteer to demonstrate one of the aspects of *FOCUS*.
2. Show both the proper and the improper ways to *FOCUS*.
3. Identify a topic of interest that you would like to discuss. Pair with a partner. Each person should spend 1 1/2 minutes sharing information and using the *FOCUS* skills.
4. Discuss how easy or difficult this exercise is.

3.03 Activity

Dominoes for Feedback

Purpose:

To illustrate the need for feedback.

Directions:

1. You will work in groups of three—a receiver, a sender, and an observer.
2. As a receiver you will create a pattern of seven dominoes and draw a new pattern of your own without anyone seeing it.
3. Seven dominoes are given to the receiver.
4. A screen is placed between the sender and the receiver.
5. The sender uses a pattern with dominoes arranged on it.
6. The sender is directed to give instructions to the receiver to place the seven dominoes in an identical pattern to the one in front of the sender without allowing the receiver to ask questions or say anything. Time limit: two minutes.
7. The observer notes the behavior and attitude expressed.
8. Repeat the process by first allowing the pairs to talk for one minute before creating a new pattern. The one minute allows time to agree on directions, common vocabulary and needed information.
9. Exchange roles. A new pattern is used once the screen is in place and you begin, *except* this time the receiver *can* ask questions and the sender can answer. You should *not,* however, look at each other.
10. The observer should share observation notes with the pair.

Discussion Questions:

1. How did you feel during the exercise as the sender? As the receiver?
    A. How did you feel not being able to ask questions?
    B. How did you feel not being able to check progress?
    C. How did you feel not being able to find out if you were being understood?

2. How did the observers feel not being able to participate?
3. Would it have been easier to have a little time at the start to:
   A. Think, plan, organize?
   B. Develop terms for the different parts of the domino, ways to describe connecting the dominoes, and so forth? What terms would you have developed?
4. Try it again using the terms developed and a new pattern.

3.04 Activity

What is Listening?

Purpose:

To check your understanding of listening.

Directions:

Do you know what listening is? You probably think you do. After all, everybody knows about listening. It's a natural part of everyday life.

But do you really know what listening is? Try this true-false quiz and see how you come out. Circle **T** for **True** or **F** for **False**.

Discuss the results of this questionnaire.

T F 1. Listening and hearing are the same thing.

T F 2. We spend only a small portion of our daily waking time taking in information.

T F 3. Most of our information comes from reading or talking, not listening.

T F 4. Bad listeners are not as intelligent as good listeners.

T F 5. Learning to read will automatically teach us how to listen.

T F 6. We think faster than we talk.

The answers are in the Appendix.

3.05 Reading Selection

Unfocused Listening

Purpose:

To demonstrate how much of your time is spent in listening and the need to be a good listener.

Directions:

Read the following and discuss:

What goes on in your head when you listen? Something like this probably.

In other words, your brain is like a whirling tornado of random thoughts and impressions. But why? Why all that confusion and lack of focus?

The answer is that your brain can think at a tremendous rate, like a computer. But the rate of human speech is only about 150 to 175 words per minute. Since your brain can handle that many words without half trying, only a part occupies itself with taking in the speaker's message. The rest goes looking for things to do. Concentration wanders away and confusion results. Another barrier is put up.

Most speeches don't give your brain enough to do to keep it occupied so your mind wanders. This misuse of spare thinking time is one of the biggest barriers to accurate listening.

During its spare time, your undisciplined brain picks up all the sounds around it. For that reason, noise interference becomes another barrier to good listening. If several people speak at once, or if background sounds are too loud, you'll have to strain to get the speakers message.

Lack of feedback and your unfocused brain are two of the barriers that keep you from listening. Lack of proper preparation for listening is still another.

If you know what you are expected to do in any situation, you can prepare yourself for the action and you can do better at it. That's true for listening too. Learning to tune in requires knowing what is expected of you. For instance, not all listening situations require the same type of listening skills.

Discussion Questions:

1. What are some of the barriers to listening?
2. Share examples of situations that have made "listening" difficult.
3. Why would listening be crucial during tutoring?

3.06 Reading Selection
Levels of Listening

Purpose:

To relate levels of listening to the tutoring situation.

Directions:

Read the following and discuss:

Level or Type of Listening

Level I	Situation
Listening in spurts-tuning in and tuning out. Half listening-following the discussion only long enough to get your chance to talk. Quiet, passive listening-listening all the time but not looking at the speaker or responding emotionally.	Being aware that other people are in the room, but doing your own thing. Waiting your turn in a doctor's office. Watching TV or listening to the radio.
Level II	
Listening for important ideas-but not participating actively in any interaction with the speaker. Narrow listening-looking at the speaker and responding, but losing important ideas through false evaluating or too selective listening.	A lecture when you know you're having a test on the material. This is the way most of you probably listen now.
Level III	
Actively listening and raising questions-taking in main ideas, watching body language, listening creatively.	This is the way you should be listening in classes, to friends—in fact, most of the time.

By knowing ahead of time what type of listening experience you are about to have, as well as what is expected of you, you will be able to increase your ability to listen.

Discussion Questions:

1. What level of listening will you most likely use during tutoring sessions?
2. What level should the tutee use?
3. How can *you* help the tutee be a better listener?
4. Practice in a listening situation, where you try to FOCUS, but there are many distractions. What are the difficulties? Can you train your mind to pay attention and listen?

3.07 Activity
Pass the Rumor

Purpose:

To provide practice in listening skills.

Directions:

1. Make a circle with your chairs.
2. Be prepared to share a rumor with the person on your left. The rumors are in the Appendix.
3. Remain very quiet until the person on your right has shared the rumor with you-as started by the leader. Then pass it on.
4. Listen to the rumor at the end of the rumor circle. The last person should repeat the rumor out loud.

Discussion Questions:

1. What differences were noted from the beginning of the rumor to the last person?
2. How do you account for this?
3. How can you apply the lesson of this exercise to tutoring?

3.08 Activity
Biography for Non-listeners

Purpose:

To provide practice in listening skills.

Directions:

1. Get into groups of four or six and sit in a circle.
2. In each group, select one member to present a one minute biography—a summary of birth to present.
3. The autobiographer should do everything possible to make the other group members listen.
4. The other group members should do everything they can to *not* listen. The only rule is that members may not leave the group to avoid listening.
5. Continue until each member gives an autobiography or until members are sufficiently disenchanted.

Discussion Questions:

Non-listeners:

1. How did you feel as a non-listener? Were you comfortable ignoring the speaker? Why or why not?
2. As a non-listener, can you recall other instances when you have demonstrated a "non-listening' attitude or behavior? What kinds of situations would encourage you to do this?

Speaker:

1. Was it difficult speaking when no one was listening to you?
2. What did you do to try to get others to pay attention to you?
3. How do you feel about having to try too hard to get others to listen to you?

Full Group:

1. Describe the feelings a tutee might have if you didn't listen.
2. What would the possible effects be of this situation?

3.09 Activity
The Happy Hooker

Purpose:

To identify inappropriate "hooking" habits.

Directions:

1. Form groups of six.
2. One person begins discussing a topic—"something exciting that has happened to me recently"—a vacation I took or something else.
3. As soon as another member of the group hears a word that reminds that person of something in one's own life, that person "hooks" into the conversation by interrupting with a "hooking phrase."
4. The second member talks about the topic until a third members hooks and so on.
5. Make a list of the "hooking phrases."

   Speaking of that...

   That reminds me...

   Glad you mentioned that...

   Oh, right, remember the time...

   Just as you were saying...

   That's like...

   Oh, that's nothing! Let me tell you...

Discussion Questions:

1. Why was this activity called the "Happy Hooker?"
2. Make a list of the "hooking" phrases you heard used.
3. Why might someone constantly use "hooking phrases?"
4. What's the danger of being a "Happy Hooker?"
5. What could you do to help eliminate someone else "hooking" you?
6. Could "hooking" be used effectively in tutoring?

3.10 Reading Selection
Act Like a Listener

Purpose:

To review listening behavior.

Directions:

Read the following and discuss:

We have two ears and one tongue in order that we may hear more and speak less.

                          Diogenes

To *be* a good listener you must *act* like a good listener. To *act* like a good listener you should:

1. Maintain good eye contact.
2. Sit attentively. Lean forward at times.
3. Look as if you are enjoying listening. Raise your eyebrows, nod your head, smile, and laugh when appropriate.
4. Ask questions. Give encouragement to the speaker with questions.
5. Appear alert, but not tense. Be patient, relaxed.
6. Relax. This is important. People like applause, attention and recognition. You can give these to the one talking by making verbal comments like:

"I see."

"That's interesting."

"Oh."

"Is that right?"

Process:

Plan a group demonstration for the class. Divide into small groups of approximately four each and design a role play that demonstrates positive listening and good attending skills. Remember: *FOCUS*.

3.11 Reading Selection
Eye to Eye Contact

Purpose:

To demonstrate the importance of eye to eye contact in tutoring.

Directions:

Read the following and discuss:

When passing a person on the street, in our culture we are taught that eye contact of only about a second is permissible. Anything longer becomes threatening or could be interpreted as a sexual overture.

Eyes do speak. Alexander Lowen in *Betrayal of the Body* writes that "more than any other single sign, the expression in the eyes of a person indicates to what extent he is in 'possession of his faculties.'"

Behavioral scientists claim that a single glance is all that is necessary between two people to tell who is most likely to dominate the relationship. Most often the person who averts the other's eyes first signals to the other a claim to the floor, the last to avert is dominate. The scientists claim 80 percent success in predicting dominance and submission between two people on the basis of first eye contact.

In our society we don't stare at people, only at nonpersons. Enemies, athletes, performers, servants and objects are okay to stare at, but not friends or strangers. In meeting someone when passing on the sidewalk, the usual pattern is to look at the person until that person is about eight feet away, then look down or away as you pass.

Practice:

Activity I

A. Pair up and add a third person to serve as a timer.

B. Stare at each other until one person averts the other's stare.

C. The timer should record the length of the stare.

Activity II

A. Everyone walk around the room until a whistle is blown.

B. At that time pair up and start a conversation about the purpose of tutoring.

C. Tape measures or yard sticks should be used to measure the distance between eyes and compare measurements.

Activity III

A. Cut out pictures of eyes from magazines or newspapers.

B. Tell as much as you can about a person from the eyes.

C. If you use prominent figures, then identify their names after the discussion.

Discussion Questions:

Regarding your eyes and eye contact:

1. What ground rules exist on elevators? Walking down the street? On crowded buses?

2. What feelings did you experience staring at someone for a lengthy time?

3. What can eyes tell you about a person?

4. How should your eyes help you communicate effectively in tutoring?

3.12 Reading Selection

Do You Know What Your Voice Reveals?

Purpose:

To demonstrate the importance of verbal control.

Directions:

It's doubtful that any other characteristic reveals as much about your character and personality as your voice does. Indeed, recent studies show that the sounds we make when we open our mouths to speak provide fascinating clues to our temperament. This is a true or false quiz to let you test your knowledge of "voice appeal" against some of science's interesting findings. Read each statement and circle **T** for **True** or **F** for **False**.

T F 1. If you have pleasant voice, chances are you are well adjusted.

T F 2. You can tell an anxious person by the sound of the voice.

T F 3. When a person's voice is played back, it has a very special effect upon that person, even when asleep.

T F 4. You can tell how rapidly a person thinks by listening to that person talk.

T F 5. The person who habitually speaks in a monotone lacks confidence.

T F 6. Most people have no idea what their voice sounds like and react with shock and surprise when they find out.

T F 7. People who have a healthy measure of self-esteem and confidence usually find it a pleasant and agreeable experience when they first hear how their voice sounds.

T F 8. Your voice reveals if you're prone to heart attack.

T F 9. It's easy to disguise your feelings when talking to someone by carefully controlling your voice.

T F 10. You can judge a person's character easier by listening to the voice over the phone than by listening to it in person.

The answers are in the Appendix.

3.13 Reading Selection
Communication of Thoughts and Feelings

Purpose:

To help you identify feeling statements.

Directions:

Read the following:

Everyone has both thoughts and feelings. It is normal and necessary to have both. As a tutor, it is important for you to be able to determine whether you are hearing a thought or a feeling statement. In your half of the helping relationship, the burden falls on you to utilize good listening skills and an ability to properly identify feelings.

Why is it so important for you to be able to tell whether someone is expressing thoughts or feelings? When someone is telling you something, but acting differently than those words indicate, you might think: "Hmmm, something is strange here." The person is acting one way and saying something else. It happens all the time. We camouflage our feelings with fancy words and try to hide things that might make us vulnerable to someone. When this happens, usually very little work gets done; the tutee may lose concentration.

So, if you can pick up on feelings when they're expressed to you, you can be a more effective and efficient tutor. How? It will be easier, because you won't feel frustrated from misunderstandings and you will eliminate the road blocks many people build when they hide feelings. You will be more effective because your tutee will learn to trust you. You will be more efficient because you will not spend half of your time trying to determine what is or is not being expressed.

It will be important for you to practice identifying statements and then deciphering what those statements mean in terms of feelings.

Directions:

1. Brainstorm words that represent feelings. List these words on the board. Everyone in the group acts out or shows the feelings. Now practice by completing the list.

2. When "listening for feelings," tutors should pretend that they are a reflective image for the speaker. In other words, do not be critical, do not preach, do not save, advise or moralize. You should reflect only feelings; thereby, allowing tutees to identify their own feelings and deal with the situation accordingly. Review the feelings list when completing this activity. Read each sentence below and identify the feeling expressed in the statement. Write the feeling on the line.

_____ 1. "I made this dress all by myself."

_____ 2. "My friend moved away yesterday. I'll never have another friend like that."

_____ 3. "I hear chuckles every time I try to sing in music class."

_____ 4. "No one ever calls me to go out on Friday night."

_____ 5. "I read at least twelve books last summer."

_____ 6. "My birthday is getting close, just ten days away."

_____ 7. "The teacher tests us on Friday and *never* prepares enough.

_____ 8. "My boss said I was lazy just because I fell asleep on the job last night."

_____ 9. "My mother drinks so much I told my friends not to come to my house."

_____ 10. "There's no hope for my grades. They were bad last quarter, they'll be that way again."

_____ 11. My dance teacher said I had a lot of talent."

_____ 12. "Maybe Dorothy will talk to me again in biology."

_____ 13. "My parents can't make me study. I can do what I want."

_____ 14. "This stuff is dumb. It's baby stuff; why should I waste my time?"

_____ 15. "How can I do everything well with two tests Friday, a basketball game, dance afterwards, a church meeting and homework?"

3.14 Activity
Roadblocks to Communication

Purpose:
To learn what roadblocks can do.

Directions:
Read the following:

You have been reading about and practicing appropriate responses that are helpful. In determining those responses that are most helpful, it is important that you be aware of some types of statements that are negative in form. They may seem to be helpful when you say them, but actually they tend to cut off your effectiveness as a helper and communicator. These statements or roadblocks are listed below and defined with an example of each.

Roadblocks

1. **Direction ordering:** to tell someone to do something in such a manner that gives the other person little or no choice.
   Example: "Get home at 9:00."

2. **Warning, threatening:** to tell the other person that certain consequences will happen if the behavior continues.
   Example: "If you are not home at 9:00, you can't go out the rest of the week."

3. **Moralizing, preaching:** to tell someone things one ought to do. Example: "Stay in school so you can get a good job."

4. **Persuading, arguing:** to try to influence another person with facts, information, and logic.
   Example: "If you drop out of school, then you can't find a good job."

5. **Advising, recommending:** to provide answers for a problem.
   Example: "If I were you, I would quit being Jim's friend and be Joe's friend."

6. **Evaluating, criticizing:** to make a negative interpretation of another person's behavior.
   Example: "You got in so late, you must have been up to no good.

7. **Praising:** to make positive evaluation of another person's behavior.
   Example: "That is the most beautiful idea I have ever heard; you are great."

8. **Supporting, sympathizing:** to try to talk the other person out of feelings or to deny another person's feelings.
   Example: "Just wait, things will be better tomorrow. Your boyfriend will change."

9. **Diagnosing:** to analyze the others' behaviors and communicate that you have their behaviors figured out.
   Example: "You're just paranoid about your loss."

10. **Diverting, bypassing:** to change the subject or to not talk about the problem presented by the other person.
    Example: "I know you are having trouble with your mom, but all I want to know is do you want to go to the movie?"

11. **Kidding, teasing:** to try to avoid talking about the problem by laughing or by distracting the other person.
    Example: "Why don't you just blow up your car since it doesn't work well?"

Directions:

1. On your own paper write an example of a statement that would be a roadblock.
2. Refer to the list of roadblocks. Decide what kind of roadblock is being used in each example provided.
3. Write the number of the roadblock on the line preceding the examples.

Roadblock Examples

_____ 1. "Girls that cry are just 'babies'; come on you don't want to be a baby-the tears are going to cause a flood."

_____ 2. "I know you have a problem with your boyfriend, but let me tell you about my girlfriend, she is super and considerate."

_____ 3. "When you come in with those watery eyes, I think you must have been smoking pot."

_____ 4. "1 feel so sorry for you that you can't learn math, you are really in bad shape, poor you...."

_____ 5. "You are the greatest artist in the whole world. Your picture is beautiful. You should get an A+."

_____ 6. "You dummy, why can't you figure out your English. Speaking is so simple and you are really stupid not to understand it."

_____ 7. "You should stop smoking because it is so bad for your health. You will probably have cancer by the time you are twenty."

_____ 8. "If you come in late tomorrow, you will be grounded for a month."

_____ 9. "Do your work!"

_____ 10. "If you don't study, you won't do well; you won't pass your tests; you'll need help and it would be so much easier if you'd just study."

_____ 11. "You're always so cute when you get mad. I love to see you pout!"

_____ 12. "What I really think is wrong here is a learning disability or maybe a problem with attention. What do you think?"

Tutoring: Learning by Helping

3.15 Activity
Using the Feeling Side: Appropriate Responses

Purpose:

To provide practice in selecting an appropriate feeling.

Directions:

Following are some basic principles that will guide you to become an effective communicator. Read each principle. Following each principle is a situation in which you should determine the most appropriate response. Circle the response which shows a feeling or affective tone.

Principle 1

When another person, whether administrator, teacher, assistant, tutor, or another student, complains to you, that person is most often seeking someone to understand feelings, and it is best to respond to the feelings instead of trying to find out the facts or to verify who did what to whom. For example, Harold complains to the teacher that his friend called him a "so and so." It is best to respond to his feelings, such as "I understand how you feel, it must have made you angry and embarrassed to be called that in front of your friends."

Situation

Student:

I don't think you gave me the right grade. I deserve a higher mark than that for all my work.

Response

Teacher A:

No, you don't. My grade book shows that based on your test scores, you got the grade you deserved.

Teacher B:

Let's discuss it after school and see how you feel about it then.

Teacher C:

You feel that you've really worked hard in this course and should be recognized for it.

Answer:

If you circled C, you are correct. In C the teacher responded not to the student's complaint about the assignment, but to the student's *feelings*.

Principle 2

People naturally have mixed feelings towards persons who have authority over them. Administrators, teachers, and students have feelings of liking and resentment at the SAME time. All people need to know that such feelings are normal and natural, and they will be spared much guilt by a calm, noncritical acknowledgment and voicing of feelings: "You seem to feel two ways about him; you like him and dislike him" rather than "You are so mixed up. One minute you like somebody, then you say you hate him. Make up your mind."

Situation

Student: Boy, that teacher in my other class really makes me mad. He's so unfair. Sometimes I wish I could really tell him what I think of him.

Response

Teacher A: You're really angry at that teacher today, but last week you seemed to get along okay. You seem to feel two ways about your teacher.

Teacher B: Being mad at him isn't going to do any good. The teacher knows best, and you should try to do what he says.

Teacher C: What happened that made you mad at him? Tell me facts.

Answer: Did you select response A? Noncritical acknowledgement of the mixed feelings that a person may have toward someone with authority is best demonstrated by verbal response A.

Principle 3

Praise of a person should deal only with one's efforts and accomplishments, not with one's character and personality. For example, instead of saying: "You are such a good teacher (or student)," it is better to praise the accomplishment itself by saying, "The students are so involved in the activities you have planned for them. You worked very hard to develop ideas for each student, and it seems to have paid off," thereby letting the other person draw individual positive ideas about one's personality.

Elizabeth Sabrinsky Foster, Ed.D.

Examples:

Helpful praise: "Your students are involved in many interesting activities."

Possible inference: "I have good ideas."

(Unhelpful praise): "You are good in the classroom. Of course, you still have a lot to learn."

Situation

Teacher
Aide: That's not my responsibility. All you've given me to do is "dirty work." When I took this job I thought I would be assisting you in some way that is more meaningful.

Response

Teacher A: I expect you to help me in whatever I ask you to do. After all, I'm the teacher, and when you do the cleaning up that gives me more professional time to spend teaching the students.

Teacher B: Don't feel that way. You're a good teacher's aide, and there's a lot to learn first before moving on to more important jobs.

Teacher C: By helping them clean up, you really helped the students learn to take good care of their materials. You served as a good model for them to follow.

Answer: C praises the person's efforts and accomplishments, thereby letting the person draw positive ideas about one's personality.

Principle 4

Discipline problems consist of two parts: angry feelings and angry acts-each part has to be handled differently. Feelings have to be identified and expressed; acts may have to be limited and redirected.

Examples:

Identifying and expressing feelings: "It looks as if you are angry today.

You feel kind of mean inside. You are angry at someone. Tell me about it."

Limiting acts: "I know you want to see how quickly you can finish your work. But the materials have to be shared by several students. Let's see if we can find something else that you can work with while you are waiting your turn."

Situation

Principal: Are you aware of the noise level in your classroom? I can hear the commotion all the way down the hall. I can't have this in my school. You will have to have better control of your class.

Response

Teacher A: I guess you're angry that we're disturbing other teachers and students. But the purpose of this activity was to have all the individuals in the class demonstrate to the other students skills they had learned best. We'll talk about doing this activity another time when we're outside and won't disturb others with our talking.

Teacher B: You shouldn't criticize my teaching abilities when you don't even know why or what our class is doing. We have a good activity planned that the students are all interested in, and want to continue with it.

Teacher C: Gosh, I'm sorry. Okay, students, stop what you're doing. Take out your textbook and let's begin the lesson for tomorrow.

Answer: Did you select A? Remember the two parts of problem solving: identifying feelings and redirecting act.

Follow-up:

- After completing each item, review each of the four principles. Write, in your **own** words, a statement which reflects your understanding of the description for each principle. In other words, actually write a principle statement for principles 1-4.

- This can be done in pairs or in small groups. Compare the statements and then select the ones most representative of the ideas expressed.

Tutoring: Learning by Helping

3.16 Skills Practice

Select The "Effective" Feeling Response

Purpose:

To provide practice in understanding why or why not a response is effective.

Directions:

Below you will find two situations. Each situation presents five different things *you could* say to your students if they presented this problem to you. Read each of the five possible statements and determine how appropriate each one is by selecting the letter of the comment defining the reason. Circle the letter that you think demonstrates a reason for the appropriate response. Be prepared to explain how appropriate each response is to the situation.

Situation 1

This excerpt is the opening remark made by a tutee immediately after seating himself in the classroom.

Tutee: Miss Jones, told me to get out of class. I don't know why. She said I couldn't come back to class until I learned to stay awake. I work at a filling station until 1:00 a.m. every night and I'm tired. Anyway, who could stay awake in here. She bores you to death.

Tutor Response 1:

"Do you have to work so much at the filling station?"

A. A useful statement to help the tutee continue talking.
B. Asks for information that is irrelevant at this time.
C. Implies understanding of the tutee's problem.
D. None of the above.

Tutor Response 2:

"What does she do that you find boring?"

A. Asks for relevant information that the tutor needs to gain understanding.
B. Ignores the implicit meaning in the tutee's communication.
C. Will help the tutee focus this thought on an important aspect of the situation.
D. Implies interest in the tutee.

Tutor Response 3:

"Going to sleep in class can get you into trouble, can't it?"

A. Is a pertinent statement because it implies that the tutor understands the tutee's problem.
B. Suggests that the tutor doesn't understand the problem.
C. Is a restatement of an obvious fact.
D. None of the above.

Tutor Response 4:

"Teachers get angry when we don't behave the way they think we should, don't they?"

A. Indicates that the tutor understands what the problem is.
B. Is an irrelevant statement.
C. Will be useful to help the tutee continue talking.
D. None of the above.

Tutor Response 5:

"Is this the first time she has called you down for sleeping?"

A. Ignores the implicit meaning of the tutee's statement.
B. Asks for inappropriate information.
C. Both A and B.
D. None of the above.

Elizabeth Sabrinsky Foster, Ed.D.

Situation 2

Taken from the first interview with a tutee who is on the brink of failing school.

Tutee:

You know it makes me so mad every time... I don't know what is wrong with this school. It seems like they are out to get me. I just keep going down in grades and everything else and it's not my fault. I don't know why they have these stupid required courses. It just doesn't make sense. Why do I have to take them when I am in agriculture?"

Tutor Response 1:

"If you put your mind to it and work and study, you could get something out of these courses which you might find useful to you later."

A. This is a reality of life which the tutee must learn.

B. Useful because it helps the tutee learn from the tutor's experiences.

C. Shows that the tutee understands what has to be done.

D. None of the above.

Tutor Response 2

"You feel that since you are in agriculture you don't need to know anything about literature and history?"

A. Focuses on the tutee's feelings.

B. Focuses on the tutee's beliefs.

C. Asks for needed information.

D. None of the above.

Tutor Response 3

"What are your aims in life?"

A. Implies the tutor understands what the tutee's problem is.

B. Asks for information that is relevant at this time.

C. Ignores the implicit meaning in the tutee's communication.

D. None of the above.

Tutor Response 4:

"What makes you think the school is out to get you?"

A. Is a pertinent question if the tutor is to understand the situation.

B. Misses a more pertinent element for exploration.

C. Suggests the tutor is interested in the tutee's point of view.

D. None of the above.

Tutor Response 5:

"It sounds to me like you're blaming others for your own inadequacies. "

A. Is a bad statement because it implies an insight beyond the tutor's awareness.

B. Is a bad statement because it focuses on an irrelevant element of the tutee's communication.

C. Is a bad statement because it makes an incorrect interpretation.

D. Is a good statement because it states a truth the tutee should recognize and accept.

A Reminder:

Select the *most effective* affective response. The following were the responses most frequently selected by a group of 200 counselors in training: Situation 1: 1B, 2B, 3C, 4C, 5C; Situation 2: 1D, 2B, 3C, 4B, 5A.

Tutoring: Learning by Helping

3.17 Activity

Tutoring Simulation: Tape the Tutor

Purpose:
To practice appropriate responses.

Directions:
1. The tutor is to read through *Script One*.
2. The tutor should then read *Script One* aloud. The tape recorder is to be turned on.
3. The tutor who is the script reader will read the student part and wait for a response.
4. After all ten responses have been given, turn off the tape, give *Script Two* to the other tutor and repeat the process.

Use:
1. We will use this as a pre and post evaluation measure on types of responses given. Though there may be no *right* answers, some responses would be better than others.
2. This will be done in the first and fourth quarter of the school year.

Situation I Script One

Student: Oh no, not this stuff again. I hate doing prefixes.
Response 1: _____
Student: I don't see why we have to do it. I've done it for the last five years.
Response 2: _____
Student: Well, Joe keeps making fun of me when we finish every day because he doesn't have to do it.
Response 3: _____
Student: I think I'll punch him out the next time he says something to me. I'll show him.
Response 4: _____
Student: If we don't do something different tomorrow, I'm not gonna do anything.
Response 5: _____
Student: I may not even come to school if we have to keep this up.
Response 6: _____
Student: Why don't we just "pretend" we're doing this and when the teacher walks up, we can break into it, like we've been doing it all along. How 'bout that?
Response 7: _____
Student: Well, if you don't make somebody move Joe, I'll move him.

Response 8: _____
Student: You better not be telling people I'm dumb.
Response 9: _____
Student: I'm as good as you-remember that.
Response 10: _____

Situation 2 Script Two

Student: I just failed my last class's test. I hate going there-I'll never pass that class. If I get yelled at again I'll walk out-and don't you start in on me.
Response 1: _____
Student: You had that class, you know what I'm talking about.
Response 2: _____
Student: Would you let someone tell you that you're stupid?
Response 3: _____
Student: Well, every time we have a test or quiz or assignment, it makes me feel so dumb. Maybe I am dumb.
Response 4: _____
Student: And then after that I have to come here. You think I can do my work here?
Response 5: _____
Student: I'm gonna have my dad come out here. He'll tell that teacher, principal and everybody off.
Response 6: _____
Student: But, if they find out I flunked that test, I won't see HBO or a movie for a month.
Response 7: _____
Student: Put that stuff away-I can't concentrate on it. I'll never be able to concentrate on it.
Response 8: _____
Student: So what? If I flunk this-it doesn't matter. I might as well, I'm flunking everything anyway. Who cares? Not me.
Response 9: _____
Student: Who are you anyway? You can't help me pass. What difference does it make if you care?
Response 10: _____

Chapter 4
Establishing Proper Behavior in Tutoring

Chapter Concepts:

1. Accepting responsibility for your own behavior can influence others to do the same.
2. You must be able to manage your own behavior before attempting to manage another's.
3. Preventive discipline measures are critical in management and increase the effectiveness of tutoring.

Chapter Objectives:

1. To help you to learn skills that will allow you to manage your personal behavior.
2. To help you to learn how to maintain a warm but monitored atmosphere for tutoring.
3. To help you to learn discipline prevention techniques, such as positive reinforcement.

Chapter Description:

This chapter will describe the skills necessary to maintain a monitored, controlled and warm environment conducive to learning. Your behavior can have an effect on your tutee. It will be important for you to determine what adjustments you might need to make to provide a relaxed but controlled situation. Positive reinforcement techniques will be studied in this chapter.

Chapter Vocabulary:

task-oriented, positive reinforcement, negative reinforcement, appropriate, disruptive, establish, strategies

Contents

4.01	You are Responsible for Your Own Behavior	Reading Selection	46
4.02	Behavior Management	Reading Selection	47
4.03	Can Emotions Affect Your Behavior?	Activity	48
4.04	Pre-Test for Positive Reinforcement	Activity	50
4.05	Definition and Examples of Positive/Negative Reinforcement	Reading Selection	51
4.06	Statements on the Application of Positive Reinforcement	Reading Selection	53
4.07	Identifying Rules for Appropriate Behavior in Tutoring	Skills Practice	53
4.08	Test Your Management in Tutoring	Activity	54

4.01 Reading Selection

You are Responsible for Your own Behavior

Purpose:
To provide a principle upon which tutoring concepts are based.

Directions:
Read the following and discuss:

Behavior Principle

I cannot be responsible for something I cannot change and that is you. I must be responsible for myself and the manner in which I conduct myself. Only you have the power to change yourself. If you will accept personal responsibility for your own behavior and I accept personal responsibility for my behavior, then together we will influence others around us to accept the same responsibility for their behavior.

Discussion Questions:

1. How can modeling behavior influence others?
2. Why must you first be responsible for your own behavior before the behaviors of others?
3. Who is in charge of *your* behavior?
4. If someone else attempted to encourage you to behave in some negative way, what choices do you have?
5. Do you have the right to tell others what to do?
6. Write your own principle of behavior.
7. Review the "Ethics for the Peer Helper" in the Appendix. Relate the ethics statement to your "principle of behavior."

4.02 Reading Selection
Behavior Management

Purpose:

To learn principles of management.

Directions:

Read the following and discuss:

One premise upon which we will base all of our behavioral attitudes in tutoring is: Each of you is responsible for your own behavior. Other people do not change you or your behavior. You do not change other people or their behavior. We may be influenced, we may ask advice and even take it, but the only person that changes you is *YOU!* That is true of everyone. Once you accept responsibility for your own attitudes and behavior, you may then be able to provide a climate that will encourage consistent positive behavior on the part of the person with whom you are working.

Your behavior and that of the tutee's greatly influences the effectiveness of each tutoring session. It is your responsibility to develop a climate that is understanding and warm as well as task-oriented. Your task is the tutoring of subject matter. The subject may vary. To accomplish the task you must use your time for tutoring to maximum benefit and not allow poor behavior to interfere with the process. By not allowing poor behavior, you must know how to encourage proper behavior and what to do if it is not exhibited consistently. This is a difficult job. A good beginning will assure a smooth middle and ending.

Because your time is limited in each tutoring session, your time on task must be complete. In this chapter you will read about:

1. How your own behavior is affected by your personal needs.
2. How emotions can affect behavior and why.
3. How positive reinforcement can be used effectively in tutoring to deter behavior problems on the part of the tutee.

Remember that all of the things you have studied so far in Chapters 1, 2 and 3 will help to prevent problems if you will work to develop all the necessary tutoring skills. Things to keep in mind from earlier chapters:

1. Knowing yourself will help you better understand others.
2. Positive self-concept building is contagious.
3. Helping relationships are developed through trust and caring.
4. We must use the most productive helping skills to assist others with change.
5. Well developed communication skills help eliminate misunderstandings and encourage positive interaction.

Preventing problems is the key to tutoring. Discipline is less an issue if the tutor continues to practice and develop the skills as listed above. Remember: problems that you prevent will never be an issue.

Be alert to potential issues surrounding your tutoring assignment. Pay attention to your tutee. Make sure the tutee is your focus of attention. Prevention of problems results from skill, caring, and positive attitudes.

Discussion:

Discuss in small groups the differences between prevention of problems and intervention once problems have occurred. Why should we focus on prevention?

Tutoring: Learning by Helping

4.03 Activity

Can Emotions Affect Your Behavior?

Purpose:

To identify emotional reactions in stress situations.

Directions:

There are times in life when emotions swing up and down, back and forth. At those times, how do you think those emotions affect how you feel about certain people? About issues? About caring? If you realize that points of stress, crisis, emotion affect your behavior, you are most likely human. There is nothing wrong in experiencing emotions. It is healthy. The problem with emotions occurs when one loses touch with what or who is in control. Will you let your feelings or emotions rule your behavior? Will you act irresponsibly because you feel badly about something? Will you make excuses for yourself because "something went wrong?"

Will you blame someone else for your mistake? If you answered yes to any of those questions, then emotions may be a problem for you. Let's see how you react to the following:

In this activity you are to examine your emotional responses to people situations. How well you are able to project yourself into these situations will determine how you might actually respond. The purpose of the activity is to determine if you can accurately and honestly describe your *first feelings* and *emotional* reactions to these situations.

Situations

1. The night is a cold and snowy one. Your mother asked you to go the drug store to pick up cough medicine for her cold. The roads are wet and slick. You look for a spot as close to the store as you can, but all the places seem to be taken. You see a spot in the waiting line, but realize that one van is half way between two outlined spaces. There's no good reason for that van to take up *two* spaces.

    A. What are your feelings about the situation?

    B. How do you feel about the driver?

    C. What would you like to say to the driver?

2. It is Thursday night and you are working on a term paper. This is the deadline and you're tired. Your only pen runs out of ink so you dash over to the closest dime store to pick up a pen refill. The cashier ignores you as you approach the counter. In fact, she picks up the phone to dial a number which she can't get. Finally you request help. She takes your money but doesn't say anything at all.

    A. What is your reaction to the situation?

    B. How do you feel about the cashier?

    C. What would you like to say her?

3. One afternoon, while driving a friend home from school, you are chatting and notice behind you that a car is blinking lights and beeping, trying to get around you. The beeping car pulls out to pass without regard for the car coming in the opposite direction. This forces you off the road. The person you saw who passed you must have been at least 80 years old.

    A. What is your reaction to the situation?

    B. How do you feel about the 80-year-old?

    C. What would you say to that driver?

4. You're at your very first concert. It's a big event and you've been waiting for a long time. As you wait in line to turn in your ticket there appears to be a delay of some type which is going to make you late. You hear some loud yelling and people moving around. The ticket taker makes no effort to hurry the line along.

    A. What's your reaction to the situation?

    B. How do you feel about the ticket taker?

    C. What do you want to say to the ticket taker?

5. You get to work one morning and notice that the manager is speaking in a rather slurred fashion and seems to forget your name. You know he's had a drink or two before, when you were on the night shift. Now he's trying to tell you that your appearance detracts from your job effectiveness.

    A. What's your reaction to the situation?

    B. How do you feel about the manager?

    C. What would you like to say to the manager?

6. You see Mrs. Smith coming down the school hall after third period with her hand tightly clenching the biology book. You say "hi," she says nothing. After fourth hour biology class has begun, you get up to ask a question and accidentally knock your book off the desk. Mrs. Smith yells, "Take your book and get down to the office, right now!"

    A. How do you react to this situation?

    B. How do you feel about Mrs. Smith?

    C. What would you like to say to her?

Elizabeth Sabrinsky Foster, Ed.D.

Rationale for Emotion

Now that you have had an opportunity to express your initial feelings about each of these situations, let's go one step further. Read on to see how each situation ended. How do your feelings change in each event once you have the additional facts?

1. You do finally get a spot to park after waiting five minutes for someone to leave. As you walk in, the driver of the van rushes out. When you get inside you hear the cashier talking about the mother who had just rushed in to get an antidote of some sort after her child had swallowed some type of poison. The mother was so upset she didn't notice how she had parked the van.

2. You call the manager the next day to report the rude behavior of the cashier. The manager tells you about the robbery that had *just* occurred before you walked in. In fact, the girl was trying to call the police and the line was busy. She was almost in shock she was so afraid. How do you feel now? Any change?

3. As you pull into your friend's neighborhood, you see a little child lying on the side of the road, with the ambulance pulled up next to the child. There also is the 80-year-old driver, the child's grandfather, who had been called after his grandson was hit by a car. How do you feel now? Any change in attitude?

4. The problem is apparent as you finally are able to move through the line, one of the ticket attendants suffered a heart attack and was unable to be moved until the EMT's arrived. Do you feel differently now? In what way?

5. You say nothing about this until you see the store owner three days later. At the time the owner tells you the manager has been sick and in fact was just hospitalized after experiencing a stroke. He had been under a great deal of stress and as a result and had not been functioning very well in his job. How do you feel about the manager now?

6. You go to the of office, quite confused. The assistant principal asks you why you deliberately dropped your book and tried to cause trouble. Still confused, you tell him you don't know what he's talking about. He tells you that for two classes, just before fourth hour, on a given cue, all the students dropped their biology books at the same time. When Mrs. Smith saw your book drop, she thought you were instigating the same situation in fourth hour. Of course you weren't, you didn't know anything about it. Does this change your feeling about Mrs. Smith? How does this information help you better understand Mrs. Smith's behavior? What would you now say?

Follow-up: "Can Emotions Affect Your Behavior?"

Aha. So *you can* let your emotions cloud your judgment. Maybe *you can* get angry, frustrated, disgusted and want to let everyone know, and *maybe* even do it. What if you do? There can be many consequences to immediate reactions to emotional situations, certainly more than we have room to name here. What you must keep in mind as a tutor is, do not let emotional situations cloud your judgment. Try to be open and nonjudgmental.

Once you become emotional, your behavior will more than likely be inconsistent and possibly create a situation more difficult to mend than if you had been able to maintain a steady profile throughout the tutoring session. You have other outlets for your emotions than through tutoring. Remember, it is your responsibility to control your behavior and provide an example for your tutee.

Now, once you have determined that you can leave your troubles outside the door, what other things can you do to insure a minimum of discipline difficulties? Following is a pretest on positive reinforcement. Positive reinforcement is a technique we will employ to strengthen positive behavior. After taking the pretest, ask for the answers. An explanation will follow.

Tutoring: Learning by Helping

4.04 Activity

Pre-Test for Positive Reinforcement

Purpose:

To determine your level of understanding of positive reinforcement.

Directions:

Complete the following questions to help you decide how well you understand the principles and procedures for implementing positive reinforcement. Circle the choice you feel is correct and check your answers with the key in the Appendix.

1. We use positive reinforcement because:
    A. It will make the tutee more comfortable.
    B. The tutor becomes a pleasant person.
    C. It will strengthen the response it follows.
    D. A positive approach is always better.

2. We've all had the experience of a certain person always blurting out the answer and spoiling the lesson for everyone else and our disposition for us. We insist that everyone raise their hands when desiring to speak. Tom often speaks without raising his hand, but today he does and we figure it's about time. Because Tom already has taken so many of the other students' turns and has blurted out so many answers, we don't call on him but instead call on someone else. Now that we have Tom quiet, we feel it is only fair to give someone else a turn. On our next question, Tom again blurts out the answer. This is probably because:
    A. Tom has had the habit so long that it will take him time to get over it.
    B. Tom has never learned to take turns.
    C. We did not reinforce the behavior we wished to reoccur.
    D. Tom is mad because we did not call on him.

3. The introduction alone of classroom rules for appropriate behavior usually:
    A. Is effective in modifying behavior.
    B. Is effective when combined with the ignoring of inappropriate behavior.
    C. Is effective when combined with the ignoring of inappropriate behavior and teacher praise for appropriate behavior.
    D. Has the effect of increasing disruptive behavior.

4. When giving praise to a student for an appropriate behavior, it is most effective when the tutor gives it:
    A. At the end of the period.
    B. Immediately following the appropriate behavior.
    C. Around five minutes later.
    D. At the end of the day.

5. When we want to change someone's behavior, the first step is to:
    A. Punish the person the first time the person behaves inappropriately.
    B. Ignore the inappropriate behavior.
    C. Don't say anything right then, but make a note to praise the person when appropriate behavior is exhibited.
    D. Identify with the student the behavior to be changed, letting acceptable and what is.

6. It is sometimes necessary to remind a person that one should stop behaving in a certain way. At that point, the best thing to do is:
    A. Punish the offender on the spot.
    B. Remind the student how good the behavior was last week.
    C. Offer a suggested alternative activity that is acceptable.
    D. Ask why the student participated in the particular behavior.

7. The rules phase of positive reinforcement should include:
    A. Overlooking the inappropriate behavior.
    B. Stating the behavior that is unacceptable.
    C. Providing a guideline for acceptable behavior.
    D. Praise for properly conducting oneself.

8. Horace has popped his gum for the second time and half of it is on his face. How should the tutor respond?
    A. Provide more gum.
    B. Ignore the entire incident.
    C. Punish Horace by refusing to allow him to chew gum.
    D. Discuss the appropriate way to chew gum in class and during tutoring.

Follow-up:

Take this test again at the end of the chapter as a post-test.

Elizabeth Sabrinsky Foster, Ed.D.

4.05 Reading Selection
Definition and Examples of Positive/Negative Reinforcement

Purpose:

To provide examples and use of positive/negative reinforcement in tutoring.

Directions:

Read the following paragraphs and discuss.

There are certain steps in using positive reinforcement techniques that you must learn in order to be an effective tutor. The technique is not complicated. You will most likely find it is the way that you would like all your teachers to reinforce you, because, it works. This technique builds on strengths and positive behavior rather than the negative. It is designed to encourage positive behavior and to make that behavior the rule rather than the exception.

Positive Reinforcement:

Using praise to reward good behavior as a means to encourage repetition of that behavior.

Negative Reinforcement:

Making a poor/degrading type of statement or action designed to eliminate the behavior just exhibited. (But, it usually doesn't eliminate it.)

Following are the three phases or steps of the positive reinforcement technique:

1. **Rules phase:** identifying specific behavior you want the students to learn. This phase consists of the tutor forming four or five rules for appropriate tutoring session behavior and repeating then four to six times a week. e.g. "Sit quietly while working, do not remove the timer," "Stay on task," and so forth.

2. **Ignore phase:** identifying specific behavior you want the students to change. This phase of the technique consists of the tutor attempting to *not* respond to (ignore) disruptive behaviors with scolding or reprimands. You are to act as if such behavior did not happen. This part of the process may be very difficult for you to follow.

3. **Praise:** identifying appropriate behaviors for which you want to give social approval. This phase consists of the tutor showing approval of as many good behaviors as possible during the first few days. A prime rule is "Catch the student being good."

Results indicate that the introduction of rules alone is not effective in modifying behavior. The procedure of ignoring inappropriate behavior is difficult for the teacher or tutor. Many ignore for a while and then scold as the students get out of hand. *Only when the tutor both praises appropriate behavior and ignores inappropriate behavior does the unacceptable behavior decline.*

Ignore disruptive behaviors unless someone is getting hurt. Focus your attention on the students who are working well to prompt the correct behaviors in the students who are misbehaving. Reinforce improvement when it does occur.

Remember: Be responsible for yourself and your behavior. Change is slow. Positive reinforcement techniques and positive responsible behavior will help produce a warm climate for learning.

Tutoring Examples of Positive/Negative Reinforcement

When you give someone praise such as "good job," "that's a great way to do it," or "you're terrific" you are using positive reinforcement. You are saying good things about some worthwhile thing another person has said or done. More than likely, the person will repeat the behavior that elicited such praise because it feels good to hear nice things. We all like to be appreciated.

If someone does something that is negative or irresponsible, a likely comment is, "you jerk, what a dumb thing to do" or "wow, are you ever stupid, where were you when brains were passed out?" Those kinds of statements tend to be humiliating, and embarrassing, but generally don't influence the person to stop, especially if the *only* way to get any attention is to do something poorly or in a negative way. The negative comments to that person then become negative reinforcers. By giving attention to something that is negative, you increase the likelihood that it will reoccur.

Let's look at a specific tutoring example:

Harold comes in to be tutored and he wants to talk very loudly. He has no intention of lowering his voice so you tell him about it. He comes in the third day and you're sick and tired of his loud voice and him and you really tell him off. You then report it to the classroom teacher. Well now Harold knows he better get down to the assignment so on the fourth day he is quiet. You are certainly relieved now. But, on the fifth day Harold starts again. Why? One possibility might be that when Harold finally did act right, no one bothered to reinforce him for the proper behavior. You might have been so glad he was finally quiet that you said nothing about it at all. In fact the only things you had said about his behavior were negative things so why shouldn't he do something that gets some attention?

Let's look at another example. This time we'll try to use the three phases of positive reinforcement.

You meet with Alexandria for several times. You establish the rule that Alexandria should remain seated by you during the entire tutoring session and not get up until the timer rings. (Phase One Rules: You must first determine what behavior you want to change.) In this case, the change is obvious: remain seated until the ringing of the bell. You must let her know that the inappropriate behavior is unacceptable. You should then remind her of the rule. Ignore (Phase Two: ignore) the disruptive behavior. Then watch for signs of appropriate behavior and praise (Third Phase: praise) her for it. Praise her if she sits longer than usual, and eventually the early rising should decrease. By using this technique, you have avoided a confrontation and provided Alexandria with more positive feelings by praising responsible behavior.

Use of punishment should be kept to a minimum whenever possible. A discussion with your supervising instructor will help determine the proper course to follow. Punishment should be determined by the teacher and carried out by the teacher. Discipline and/or punishment are *not* the responsibility of the tutor.

Read the following situation and then determine what should be done using positive reinforcement:

Jenny and her boyfriend, Northrup, sit on separate sides of the room; however, during the tutoring lesson, Northrup's seat is one away from Jenny. For the first few minutes of tutoring each day, Northrup seems to pay attention, but shortly thereafter you hear whispers coming a seat away and Northrup is constantly distracted. He seems to make pretty good tutoring grades, but you think he could do better. In fact on two days when Jenny had the flu he made 95s.

Discussion Questions:

1. To have an effective tutoring session, what behavior can you identify that needs to be changed?
2. What rule would you establish to alert Northrup to the problem?
3. How would you carry out Phase Two?
4. What behavior would you ignore?
5. What types of praise might be appropriate for Northrup?
6. What positive reinforcers might you make do?
7. How might you tell when change occurs?

4.06 Reading Selection

Statements on the Application of Positive Reinforcement

Purpose:

To summarize statements applicable to positive reinforcement.

Directions:

Read the following statements and discuss.

1. We use positive reinforcement because it will strengthen the response it follows.
2. A positive reinforcer can be anything that is desired or needed by the student.
3. If the teacher or tutor does not praise appropriate behavior, the effect is to increase the disruptive behavior.
4. Prescribing behavioral rules alone is relatively ineffective in changing behavior.
5. It is important how the teacher/tutor behave.
6. Catch the student being good
7. Teacher's tutor's praise is important in maintaining a well functioning classroom.
8. It is not the total amount of praise given by the teacher/tutor which is important for the good classroom management, but when and to whom the praise is given.
9. Just being nice is not enough.
10. Criticisms are found not to function as punishers but as reinforcers for misbehavior.
11. Learning not to respond to disruptive behavior is important for effective teaching.
12. "Ignore" is a key word.
13. Often our attempt to correct students by telling them what *not* to do fails.
14. If we help to develop students' intellectual competencies at the expense of their self-esteem we have failed!

Follow-up:

1. Brainstorm in small groups a list of all the ways you can say "good job!"
2. Discuss "ignoring" techniques.
3. Analyze what techniques motivate you to do what is expected.

4.07 Skills Practice

Identifying Rules for Appropriate Behavior in Tutoring

Purpose:

To provide practice in using the three phases of positive reinforcement in tutoring.

Directions:

Make a list of no more than four rules you feel are necessary for appropriate behavior in tutoring sessions. Don't consult with anyone prior to writing your list.

Rule 1: _____

Rule 2: _____

Rule 3: _____

Rule 4: _____

Develop strategies to encourage the behavior you desire for each rule. How would you use positive reinforcement to encourage the maintenance of the behavioral rules? List as many different ways as possible.

1. _____
2. _____
3. _____
4. _____
5. _____
6. _____
7. _____

Work in groups of four and compare rules and strategies.

Now, retake the *Positive Reinforcement Pre-Test* and evaluate your understanding of this technique.

Tutoring: Learning by Helping

4.08 Activity

Test Your Management in Tutoring

Purpose:

To provide "real" situations you may have to confront.

Directions:

The best approach to discipline is a preventive one. Positive reinforcement is one of the strongest approaches used. By practicing the techniques introduced previously you will probably minimize your discipline problems; however, an occasional problem may arise, This does not indicate lack of training or ability on your part, but rather that you cannot control all situations. By considering certain problem areas early, you may be better prepared to handle them, should they occur. Think about these possibilities and answer these two questions for each situation given:

1. What is your responsibility should the situation occur?

2. What would you do if the situation did occur?

Situations:

A. If a tutee is involved in cursing or an obscene gesture?

B. If a tutee steals something?

C. If a tutee shouts at you angrily and threateningly?

D. If a tutee ignores you while working.

E. If a tutee refuses to cooperate?

F. If a tutee leaves the session?

G. If a tutee cheats on his answers?

H. If a tutee hides a test?

I. If a tutee strikes you or another student?

J. If a tutee speaks too loudly?

K. If a tutee is always tardy to the session?

L. If a tutee continued to distract others in the classroom?

M. If another student distracted your tutee?

N. If the tutee is continually absent from school?

Chapter 5
Principles of Education as Applied in Tutoring

Chapter Concepts:

1. People learn in different ways; knowing how will increase tutoring effectiveness.
2. Understanding basic principles of learning allows you to understand structure and procedure.

Chapter Objectives:

1. To provide a foundation of principles upon which you will base tutoring work.
2. To determine your attitude about education.
3. To help you to learn strategies that allow maximum learning to take place in minimal time.

Chapter Description:

This chapter is an overview of basic principles that deal with use of time, effective practice and means by which people learn. It is important to know why we do what we do. This chapter will help you analyze tutoring structures and techniques.

Chapter Vocabulary:

principles, motivation, concrete experience, self-motivated, meaning, modeling, monitoring, accuracy, fluency, proficiency, ineffective

Contents

5.01	Why Study Principles?	Reading Selection	56
5.02	The School Line	Activity	57
5.03	Principles Dealing with How Students Learn Best	Reading Selection	57
5.04	Principles Dealing with Instructional Time	Reading Selection	58
5.05	Principles Dealing with Effective Practice	Reading Selection	59
5.06	Fundamental Questions Asked About Effective Practice	Reading Selection	60

5.01 Reading Selection

Why Study Principles?

Purpose:

To provide a purpose for studying basic principles of education upon which tutoring concepts are based.

Directions:

Read the following material and discuss.

"Know thyself."

Socrates

The following excerpt is from *Hope for the Flowers*.

. . . Full of agitation Stripe asked a fellow crawler: "Do you know what's happening?" "I just arrived myself," said the other. "Nobody has time to explain; they're so busying trying to get wherever they're going up there." "But what's at the top?" continued Stripe. "No one knows that either but it must be awfully good because everybody's rushing there. Good-bye; I've no more time!" He plunged into the pile....

It is through education and the foundation of it that we seek the truth of "what's at the top."

Principles provide us with a foundation upon which to design and develop programs of instruction. It is through those principles that we attempt to set and teach goals. It is because of those principles that we are able to understand why and how people learn.

Education is not something that just happens. It takes thought, planning, work, exposure, opportunity, interest and challenge. The uniqueness of each individual provides a true challenge for those in the business of education.

It's not enough to rush to the top without knowing *why*! Therefore we study educational principles.

"Until thought is linked with purpose there is no intelligent accomplishment."

James Allen

*I listen and forget
I read and understand
I see and remember
I do and I learn.*

Oriental Proverb

*It never has been
It is not now,
It never shall be,
What you teach,
But **how** you choose to share it
That will make the difference.*

Elizabeth Foster

Discussion:

1. Compare the quotes listed. What do they have in common?
2. Get a copy of *Hope for the Flowers* and read it to gain the full benefit of the message. What is the moral of the story?

Chapter 5 — Principles of Education as Applied to Education

5.02 Activity
The School Line

Purpose:

To determine your attitudes about learning and school.

Directions:

1. Take a length of heavy yarn or string that represents your school life.
2. Take one 3 x 5 card for each two years you have spent in school.
3. On each card write events or feelings you remember from each year in school. One side per year. The events, feelings and people can be either positive or negative.
4. After writing each event, go back and place a gold star by each positive experience.
5. Draw dark lines or marks around the experiences that were not positive.
6. After the cards are ready, punch holes in the top corner of each one, slip them onto the string and staple or knot them in place.

This is an opportunity to review attitudes about school. This represents the school line. Review the groups' cards to see if there are more stars or black lines. Share your experiences.

Remember:

Everyone comes to you with a school line. It's important to know whether that person has many gold stars or only a few.

Reactions:

A. How can your school life experiences affect your attitude toward school?
B. How can your attitude about school affect your ability to tutor?
C. How can your attitude about school affect your ability to work with teachers?
D. How can you assure yourself that this year's card will be full of stars?
E. How can you assure your tutees that their card for this year will have some stars?

5.03 Reading Selection
Principles Dealing with How Students Learn Best

Purpose:

To instruct you in how people learn best and to help you apply that information to the tutoring situation.

Directions:

Read the following and discuss.

Students learn best when:

1. They are actively motivated.
2. They have concrete experiences.
3. They have options.
4. They are satisfying their own interests and needs.
5. They are accepted for their own learning style and rate.
6. They are succeeding.
7. They have good self-concepts.
8. Their objectives are used.
9. They are self-motivated.

Consider how you can assist others as a tutor by using these principles.

Discussion Questions:

1. How can you actively motivate tutees?
2. How can tutees have concrete experiences in tutoring? What does "concrete" mean?
3. How can you give tutees options and what kinds?
4. How will you help the tutees satisfy their interests?
5. How will you demonstrate you have accepted the tutees' learning style(s)? Name some different learning styles.
6. How will the tutees succeed in tutoring?
7. How will you encourage the tutees to form good self-concepts?
8. How can you incorporate the tutees' learning objectives in tutoring?
9. How can the tutees be self-motivated in tutoring and how will you encourage that?

5.04 Reading Selection
Principles Dealing with Instructional Time

Purpose:

To teach the importance of wise use of time in instruction.

Directions:

Read the following paragraphs and discuss.

Using time wisely in the classroom is a prerequisite to effective and efficient instruction. Student energy should not be devoted to wasting time through meaningless activity. The following concepts, based on work by Madeline Hunter, are as applicable in the tutoring situations as they are in any instructional program.

1. **Student time and energy should not be wasted on material that is either too difficult or too easy.**

It is a serious teaching/tutoring error to require students to work on an objective that is beyond their ability to master. It is also a serious error to require students to work on an objective that has already been mastered. Both situations result in extreme frustration for students and likely turn into meaningless time spent on meaningless activities.

2. **Student time and energy should not be spent in inefficient or ineffective methods.**

Inefficient use of time involves either too little time on an objective or too much; either of which results in student frustration. Ineffective methods would involve techniques that don't work with particular students, but because students are given no alternative, they waste time. An example might be: "Write that vocabulary word 35 times." The student might not learn the meaning of the word by writing it 35 times. That is ineffective use of time. The student might already know it after the first time. That is inefficient use of time.

3. **Student time and energy should not be devoted to tasks that are meaningless or worthless.**

Students become very frustrated very quickly when they have to spend their time doing something that seems trivial or has no application to their needs. An example of this type of error would be: "Copy the first five pages of the dictionary for homework tomorrow."

4. **Student time and energy should not be wasted by waiting for the instructor to begin instruction.**

It is very difficult to regain attention once it is lost. The instructor should not require the students to wait for papers to be passed out, wait for roll to be taken, or wait for directions to begin. Waiting encourages daydreaming and attention on activities not related to instruction.

The previously listed four principles are important to remember to ensure wise use of instructional time in classrooms. They are Important to the tutor in considering the necessity of utilizing instructional time in tutoring to the fullest. You may wonder how tutoring can effectively eliminate student waste of time and energy. If you will keep in mind what should be done in tutoring instruction as listed below you will see how tutoring can eliminate student waste of time and energy.

1. The material used in tutoring should be appropriate to the academic need of the student, level of achievement and challenge.

2. Tasks assigned in tutoring should be completed as requested. The quality of the work should be high. Use of time should be highly structured so as to use the allotted time efficiently. Methods employed during the sessions will be based on proven principles and subject to review at all times.

3. Tasks assigned should be challenging, not boring and meaningless with little application. There should be long range benefits.

4. Time spent during tutoring sessions will be on task. Wait time should be negligible.

5.05 Reading Selection
Principles Dealing with Effective Practice

Purpose:
To teach importance of effective practice as it relates to tutoring instruction.

Directions:
Read the following material and discuss.

"Practice Makes Perfect" is not necessarily so. Madeline Hunter, in her work on effective practice, states that performance can actually deteriorate as a result of ineffective practice. Because tutoring involves a great deal of "practice" for students, it is important for the tutor to know what is necessary to provide effective means of practice.

Before a new skill activity, lesson, or objective is complete, the tutor must provide the "3 M's."

The "3 M's" are:
1. Meaning
2. Modeling
3. Monitoring

What is Meaning?

Meaning is understanding what is being taught in the tutoring session. Meaning is being able to associate the instruction to some past experience or previous knowledge which will enable the student to learn more quickly. The understanding of new material depends a great deal upon how much you already know about it.

All tutoring sessions that involve the introduction of new material should begin with a check on the tutee's understanding and past experiences in relation to the material.

What is Modeling?

Modeling is the demonstration of correct responses for a lesson or objective. The tutor should demonstrate the type of answer that the student should give regardless of whether it is English, math, spelling or science. The tutor should "model" the acceptable type or form of answer expected. Always give an example of what you expect.

What is Monitoring?

Monitoring is overseeing the accuracy of the responses. It is very important in tutoring that the tutee provide accurate answers and that the tutee know what is accurate or inaccurate. If an error is practiced over and over, it is much harder to eliminate than if it is dealt with early in instruction. An example might be: Student X continues to get incorrect answers while working problems in fractions. Though the answer is wrong, the major problem is that a crucial step was continually left out during the calculation process. If the tutor "monitors" closely and catches the error during computation, it will be less likely to occur regularly.

Follow-up:
Review the descriptions associated with the principles of instructional time (5.04) and effective practice (5.05). List the questions you have about these principles and how they would apply in a tutoring situation. Put these questions on a chart pad to be sure that they are answered before this chapter is completed.

Tutoring: Learning by Helping

5.06 Reading Selection

Fundamental Questions Asked About Effective Practice

Purpose:

To determine effective practice techniques.

Directions:

Read the following material and discuss.

There are four fundamental questions about practice that are often asked and must be considered in order to plan an effective practice period. They are:

1. How much of a task should be practiced in one practice period?
2. How long should that practice period be?
3. How close together should those practice periods be scheduled?
4. How will the learner know how the results of performance?

Look at some basic principles that have been validated.

1. How much of a task should be practiced in one practice period?

The smallest amount of a task that retains maximum meaning is all that should be practiced at one time.

We would not attempt to learn a long poem all at once. We would learn it one stanza at a time or even work on just a few lines of that stanza. We would not hand learners the 100 number facts and say, "learn them!" First we would establish meaning so they understand what they are doing as they add or multiply, and then they would practice responding quickly to only a few facts. After they learned those, they would practice some additional ones.

Common examples of misuse of this principle of working on small amounts are:

A. Working on twenty spelling words in one period.

B. Studying all the number facts that have been missed (assuming there are more than 35).

C. Trying to learn everything that was missed on a test in one practice period.

Long practice periods usually are ineffective and inefficient.

2. How long should each practice period be?

Short, intense, highly motivated practice periods produce more learning which is better remembered than long drawn out periods. Of course, the practice period must be long enough to get something done, but not so long that attention and effort wane from fatigue or loss of interest. It is amazing what a few minutes spent on highly motivated practice will produce in a student's learning and remembering. Short intense practice periods several times a day will produce more learning than double that amount of time at one setting.

It is possible to expend too much time on ineffective or unmotivated practice. Common errors are:

A. Writing a spelling word 20 times.

B. Studying number facts for half an hour.

C. Doing 25 of the same kind of problems.

Obviously, the more complex the task, the longer it takes to do it. Practicing the writing of introductory paragraphs will take more time than the time needed to practice three spelling words. The length of the practice period must be tailored to the kind of task and the maturity of the learner. Highly skilled performers who spend many hours on practice, still practice one thing intensively for short periods.

For some tasks, 10-20 minutes may be necessary. If more time is needed, often it is better to break the task into parts, each of which is practiced for a short period. Later when each part is learned, a longer period may be needed to put them together.

3. How close together should practice periods be scheduled?

Many practice periods close together should be scheduled at the beginning of learning. This massing of practice results in fast learning. Once something has been learned, practice periods should be scheduled farther and farther apart. This distributing of practice results in long retention of the material that has been learned. When something new is introduced, there should be several brief practice periods within a short period of time (massing practice). Other practice periods should occur' during that day and on subsequent days. Once something has been learned, a review once a week and then once a month (distributing practice) will more nearly ensure remembering.

Misuses of this principle:

A. Taking a spelling test on Friday with no further attention to those words in subsequent weeks.

B. Becoming familiar with an episode in history and then moving on, never reviewing or reconsidering that episode.

C. Reading a book or article, never reviewing what it was about, and soon it's forgotten.

Working on smaller amounts of a task in a short practice period encourages massing of practice. For example, if a student is working on four number facts, each of those can be practiced many times (massed) in one minute practice periods. After they are learned, reviewing those facts twice a week, once a week and then once a month (distributed) will more nearly ensure their being remembered.

When practicing reading, it is important to mass practice on any word missed. Usually students should reread the sentence that contains the word that was missed. At the end of the page, they should go back to that word and read it again. If it isn't remembered, they should reread the whole sentence for a clue. At the end of the story they should again read any words missed to make sure they are remembered. It is helpful to make a list of missed words with the page number on which each word occurred so the students can mass practice by working on them several times that same day. The next day they should reread them and relearn any that have been forgotten. If a student is missing more than 23 words on a page, that book is too hard for reading instruction (too much needs to be learned in one practice period.) The student should change to a book in which it is possible to learn, each day, the unknown words.

4. How will students know how well they are doing?

The more immediate the knowledge of results, the easier it is for the student to improve performance or correct errors. Consequently, the student must have access to knowledge of results, either from written material or from a person as immediate feedback. Without this, practice is seldom effective.

Frequent monitoring of students when they are practicing enables quick identification of any student who needs help. Monitoring also gives successful students knowledge of results ("That's right," "You're getting them all," "That's coming along well") which in turn increases their motivation to learn.

A test becomes a highly motivated practice period when the student learns, as soon as possible after a test, what was right and, if something was missed, what the answer should have been. Violations of the principle of knowledge of results occur when papers aren't checked or tests aren't returned for several weeks or not at all.

In summary, a great deal of learning time can be saved by introducing all practice with the "3 M's": meaning, modeling, and monitoring and then by applying the four principles of effective practice:

1. Practice small meaningful parts and add more only when those are learned.

2. Schedule short intense practice periods where the student is highly motivated to "do it better."

3. Mass practice periods at the beginning so the material is learned quickly. Then distribute practice so it is long remembered.

4. Enable the student to get knowledge of results while practicing or as soon as possible afterwards.

As a tutor your job is to encourage by helping tutees to be right, letting them know when they are right, helping them to realize when they have learned, what they have learned and what they still need to practice. Your support, approval and reinforcement will help them develop more confidence in themselves so eventually they can become their own teachers and design their own practice periods-something they will need as an assist to learning throughout their lives.

Do's and Don'ts

Directions:

Review the Do's and Don'ts of effective practice that follow:

1. **Do** work on short meaningful units.

   Don't work on a long unrelated series.

2. **Do** work for short concentrated periods.

   Don't drag out practice periods.

3. **Do** review something a student learned with you previously that worked.

   Don't skip an opportunity to review previously learned material.

4. **Do** practice something new in many different contexts.

   Don't practice something new only once.

5. **Do** have a student practice something several times while you are there.

   Don't have a student learn something new and then not check to see that it is remembered.

6. **Do** give a student knowledge of results.

   Don't leave students wondering how they did.

Your Goal:

To be able to demonstrate effective practice techniques by practicing all the do's of effective practice during tutoring sessions.

Follow-up:

1. Refer to your list of questioned placed on chart paper from 5.05. Review the questions to be sure that they have all been answered.
2. Make a *Do List*. Put the "Do" items on 5 x 7 cards and place in a work folder to remind you.
3. Add other Do's that you think would be helpful that are reflected in this chapter.
4. Design activity cards with situations that you can role play to demonstrate the Do's and Don'ts. Have other students observe the role play as it is acted out. Determine what is a Do and what is a Don't.

Chapter 6
Roles, Responsibilities and Procedures in Tutoring

Chapter Concepts:

1. Demonstrating positive personal characteristics will result in successful tutoring experiences.
2. Understanding what is expected will enable you to meet expectations in tutoring.
3. Accepting assigned tutoring responsibilities will enable the program to proceed as designed.

Chapter Objectives:

1. To determine your role and responsibility as a tutor and the part that role plays in education.
2. To explore your views of school and people as they relate to the role of tutor.

Chapter Description:

This chapter provides an opportunity for the tutor to identify teacher and teaching characteristics important to education as well as an opportunity to explore responsibilities associated with tutoring. The general procedures for tutoring are introduced in this chapter.

Chapter Vocabulary:

spatial, characteristics, confidentiality, crucial, atmosphere, calculate, abide

Tutoring: LEARNING by Helping

Contents

6.01	It's Great to be Right-It's Okay to be Wrong	Reading Selection	65
6.02	What Makes a Good Teacher?	Activity	66
6.03	Logistical Concerns of Tutoring	Reading Selections	67
6.04	Characteristics That Lend to Successful Tutoring	Activity	68
6.05	Working with the Supervising Teacher	Reading Selection	69
6.06	Tips of the Tutoring Trade	Reading Selection	70
6.07	Responsibilities Chart	Reading Selection	71
6.08	What Should You Do If?	Skills Practice	72
6.09	First Meeting	Skills Practice	72
6.10	How to Begin a Lesson	Reading Selection	73
6.11	How to Handle Right and Wrong Answers	Reading Selection	74
6.12	Structure of the Tutoring Session	Reading Selection	75
6.13	Tutoring Procedures	Reading Selection	76

Chapter 6 — Roles, Responsibilities and Procedures in Tutoring

6.01 Reading Selection
It's Great to be Right—It's Okay to be Wrong

Purpose:

To provide information on why it's okay to say, "I don't know."

Directions:

Read the following and discuss:

Somewhere, way back in my early education, I know I heard, "As a teacher you know everything, or should, or should pretend to, or pretend you didn't hear the question." It was a fine line, until I started to teach. The first day, there was so much I didn't know. I couldn't pretend at all, not unless I wanted my classes to think I was completely deaf and dumb! Well, it wasn't quite that bad, but there was a lesson to be learned, and I've learned it over and over again.

E. Foster

Teachers Don't Know Everything

Let's start out with that statement and build on it. Who is a teacher? Well, there are teachers in the schools that have certificates that say they are teachers. There are principals who teach as well. There are older brothers and sisters in our schools that teach their younger brothers and sisters every day, just by being role models as well as actively teaching them how to do and say things. Most youngsters learn to ride bikes, climb trees, and play house from older brothers, sisters, mothers or fathers.

How about those mothers and fathers? What do they teach? Not such important things really, except how to talk, how to eat, walk, dress, love and live in society. The first teachers we meet in life are our parents. Parents teach us about social mores and morals.

We are taught about religion and beliefs from pastors, ministers, rabbis, priests, and the like. We are taught by anyone who knows something we don't know, that we want to know. Can every teacher know everything? The answer is too simple (of course not) but, the problem isn't that simple.

We are all always growing, always learning, always teaching, and should always be able to say, "I don't know."

Can you say, "I don't know, *but I'll* find out?" Let's look at what might make it difficult to say that.

What does or "could" it mean to someone when you say "I don't know?" It could mean: Dumb? Stupid? Overpaid? Under-educated? Expert? Not prepared? Wrong job? Unread? Untrained? All of these things run through our minds. If we subscribe to any of them, negative feelings and insecurities will creep in. We think, "Well, if I say, I don't know, someone might think I *should* know and then they'll think I'm not doing my job or that I'm not smart enough to do it." And so, that person "pretends" to know or "ignores" the question, but truly, that person has ignored the whole issue.

As teachers, in any capacity, we need to know what our responsibility is towards the issue of "knowing and not knowing." It again is simple. Be honest. Our responsibility is "Do not pretend." Be willing to say, "I don't *know, but* I'll find out." You are human. Don't be afraid to let someone else find out. We are all learners.

Remember, that in your job as a tutor you will hear, "I don't know" many times from your tutees. They will have to say that because they *can't* pretend. The evidence is too clear. Their faith and trust in you will strengthen if they hear, "I don't know" when you really don't. It doesn't indicate stupidity, it indicates honesty. In your situation, it offers the best lesson that a teacher can teach-learn from each other. We are all learning from each other. That's how we grow. I have something to offer you and in return you have something to offer me. Saying "I don't know," in that context is an "open invitation" to learning for everyone. Try to accept that invitation-practice honesty-and learn from others.

In the following pages you will have an opportunity to explore what you think makes a good teacher as well as the logistical items such as space, attendance and planning that join together to support the teacher's task of teaching. Remember that the job of tutoring is essentially a teaching job. Those characteristics you value in the "good teacher" are the same characteristics you should try to develop in your teaching role as a tutor.

Discussion:

Think of a time when you were asked something that you didn't know. How did it make you feel? Imagine that you were asked in front of 100 people, in front of 10 people, and in front of one person. How do your feelings change? If you are given time to FIND the answer, do your feelings change? How does this relate to tutoring?

Tutoring: Learning by Helping

6.02 Activity

What Makes a Good Teacher?

Purpose:
To look critically at characteristics associated with teaching.

Directions:
1. Read the following list carefully.
2. Try to determine what characteristics listed below are most important to be a *good teacher*.
3. Put them in order, the most important No. 1 and so on. Place the numbers on the blank in front of the letter.

Teacher's ability to:

____ A. Communicate effectively with students

____ B. Understand feelings of students

____ C. Listen to other people's opinion

____ D. Dress neatly and attractively

____ E. Keep order in the classroom

____ F. Be fair when disciplining

____ G. Be informed on the latest information in subject area

____ H. Use many different methods (films, records, books)

____ I. Expect high levels of achievement from students

____ J. Be liked by students

____ K. Cooperate with students' wishes

____ L. Communicate effectively with parents

____ M. Admit to error if a mistake is made

____ N. Keep good records

Follow-up Directions:
1. Form groups of approximately 4 - 6 people.
2. Compare lists and try to agree upon a priority list of important characteristics. Reach a consensus on the top five.
3. Report your group's decisions to the entire class.
4. Discuss why it might have been difficult to reach a consensus.
5. What differences existed in the groups' priorities? Why?
6. Compare your lists to a list compiled by teachers.
7. What differences and similarities exist?

6.03 Reading Selection
Logistical Concerns of Tutoring

Purpose:

To provide information upon which you can base decisions regarding space, attendance and planning.

Directions:

Read the following and discuss:

Space? How Much and Where?

Where and how should you sit? There have been numerous studies done on the effect of room arrangement and the seating of each person to the ability to relate to others; as well as the effect of nearness (spatial arrangement) on one person to another. The results of these studies have shown that for helping relationships with a one-to-one ratio, a seating arrangement with both people side by side is most desirable. The "helping" attitude is conveyed more easily next to the person you're working with as opposed to working across from each other. Working across from each other tends to suggest an authoritative posture on the part of the tutor.

Space

Space is another issue to consider. Too much space tends to create distance, vagueness, a lack of interest and caring. Too little space, such as direct contact, i.e. touching, may create a feeling of uneasiness or anxiousness. Many people need to be able to move freely without physical contact. Therefore, in the tutoring situation, we will strive for a "comfortable" distance, side by side, that encourages communication and a free-flowing direct line. Try different distances as you sit together to determine what is comfortable for both parties of the relationship.

Attendance

This critical issue is a topic that can lead to success or failure. You must be here! There is no substitute for you! There is no way that someone else can make your "tutee" feel as cared about as you can, because you have spent the time building rapport and the relationship upon which your work is based.

Occasionally, a field trip or school meeting will occur that you will want to attend. In these cases, you will know ahead. Be sure that you tell each tutee "ahead" also. They should know that you will not be there and why, just as you will want to know ahead of time, when and why your tutees won't be there.

Illness is, of course, unavoidable. Be sure to drink lots of orange juice. However, if that doesn't keep you out of the sick bed, then do your best to come as soon as you are well. Let your tutees know that you missed the sessions and again, why you were out. This small piece of information will add to your credibility and sincerity.

You are the model. You set the pace and criteria for excellence. It is important that each of your students know that being with them is worthwhile. Poor attendance on your part can do nothing but convince your students that they are unimportant to you and that the tutoring sessions are even less important. You must be dependable. Someone else's learning depends on it.

There is no replacement for you as a caring person!

Don't Get Caught With Your Plans Down!

When you think about the word plan, the P in plan can stand for poor or perfect. Though we may never actually be perfect, we can strive for excellence. Striving to be poor is not much of a contest and one you wouldn't want to win. For us, the P in plan will mean striving for perfection or as near as we can get to it. If you think ahead—plan ahead—you won't get caught with dead air in your head or your plans down!

Planning takes time.

Planning takes effort.

Planning takes initiative.

Planning takes a concerned individual.

Success takes planning!

Sure, you'll hear someone say, "Oh, I just 'winged' it for the day," or "Who knows the difference? I got through it." Believe me, people know the difference and so will your tutees.

In your capacity as a tutor, you are a teacher, a helping person. Good teachers don't "wing it." They don't take chances with something as important as someone's learning and living to just "make it through."

Planning can be time consuming. Many times, because we aren't sure what we want to do, we flounder for minutes or hours while "preparing" for teaching. Because of lack of direction we can become frustrated, accomplish little, and are less likely to tackle the "planning" process again. Self-discipline and utilization of planning time will shorten your total time spent, make you more effective in your role, and relieve frustration.

Tutoring: Learning by Helping

The Planning Formula

Consider the following steps before you begin to plan:

1. Set a time limit.
2. Decide what you want to accomplish and how you are going to do it.
3. Begin work within your time constraints.
4. Assess your product at the end of the time.

You will find that the more you practice this, the more you will accomplish in a short period of time. By defining your task and the time in which you are to accomplish it, you have enabled yourself to manage your time effectively and efficiently, thus making good use of planning and your ability to implement. It is always evident when planning takes place. It is just as evident when *no* planning takes place.

Planning time for tutoring should be set aside for such tasks as game learning, game management, material development, and learning identified skills. You will feel more confident in your ability to use your time on task more efficiently through planning.

Remember the steps to the Planning *Formula*:

1. Set a time limit.
2. Decide *what* you want to accomplish and *how*.
3. Begin your work within the time limit.
4. Assess the product at the end of your time.

Continue practicing the *Planning Formula* and you will find that time is something you manage instead of it being something that manages you! Make the P in plan mean "perfect" for you.

Follow-up:

1. Identify something for which you need to plan in preparation for your tutoring experience.
2. Use the *Planning Formula* as one method to identify steps for your planning.
3. Write your plan and assess the likelihood of its success.

6.04 Activity

Characteristics that Lead to Successful Tutoring

Purpose:

To determine characteristics most important to successful tutoring.

Directions:

List below in priority order from 1 to 15 the letters of the characteristics you think would be most important for successful tutoring.

_____ A. Ability to encourage!
_____ B. Ability to be patient.
_____ C. Ability to withhold personal opinion.
_____ D. Ability to accept people as they are, where they are, and like them for it.
_____ E. Ability to use good listening habits.
_____ F. Ability to demonstrate self-discipline.
_____ G. Ability to demonstrate a sense of humor.
_____ H. Ability to admit to error and ask for assistance.
_____ I. Ability to be dependable.
_____ J. Ability to plan and be prepared.
_____ K. Ability to respect confidentiality.
_____ L. Ability to be in attendance.
_____ M. Ability to share information.
_____ N. Ability to keep good records.
_____ O. Ability to cooperate in the classroom.
_____ P. Ability to deliver content information.

Once you have established your priority list, work in a small group of 4 - 5 and identify the group's top five characteristics.

Comparison:

Compare *Activity 6.02* with this activity and determine how many characteristics important to successful tutoring are also important to the successful teacher. Make a list of the similarities. Discuss why there may be some differences. Try to reach a group consensus.

Chapter 6 — Roles, Responsibilities and Procedures in Tutoring

6.05 Reading Selection

Working with the Supervising Teacher

Purpose:

To provide information on the role of the supervising teacher.

Directions:

Read the following material and discuss.

As a tutor you will be assigned to a room, to students, and to a teacher or teachers. This teacher will serve as a supervisor of tutor activities. What does this supervision involve?

Each supervising teacher has an opportunity to observe the tutoring process and to be involved in training on "how to use" tutors. Each teacher has read the tutor's handbook and will have an instructor's guide.

Though tutors are assigned to different tutoring grades, subjects, and instructors, the management for tutoring will remain similar in most areas.

The tutor will be responsible for keeping accurate and up-to-date records. The supervising teacher can and will at any time, check these records. These records are maintained and completed to insure that the tutee's progress can be evaluated at any time. This allows for the proper materials to be assigned and skills to be stressed. The selection of skills to be tutored is the teacher's responsibility, not the tutor's.

Specific problems in tutoring can be discussed with the supervising teacher. If these problems would be beneficial for other tutors to hear, share these situations at the training session.

The supervising teacher has requested tutors in the classroom. You are requested. The instructor feels just as you, that a valuable service is offered through tutoring and that as a team, you can provide quality assistance to students needing extra support.

By working cooperatively in the classroom, you will maintain a positive rapport with the instructor and provide a warm and stable environment in which learning can take place. Decisions about classroom management and discipline are left to the teacher. Your responsibility is to carry out tutoring assignments and to work effectively and efficiently without any added burden to the supervising teacher. Your role is to help.

Cooperation between supervising teacher and tutor is a must for the success of the program and all components of it. Be sure to do your part.

Discussion:

1. What questions do you have about your relationship with the supervising teacher?
2. What questions do you have about your responsibilities and the responsibilities of the supervising teacher?

Follow-up:

Meet with the supervising teacher to discuss expectations, records, student needs, and your plan for on-going communication.

6.06 Reading Selection

Tips of the Tutoring Trade

Purpose:

To review guidelines and responsibilities in tutoring.

Directions:

Review the following tips. These items will provide you with the guidelines necessary to function effectively as a tutor.

1. Determine your own attitudes about school, teachers, teaching and learning. Be sure not to allow them to influence your behavior during a tutoring session in any negative way.
2. Try to be informed about the interests of your "tutees" before you begin working with them. (Use an interest survey.)
3. Confer with the supervising teacher regularly to determine appropriate activities for each student and to assess the progress of each student.
4. Give your tutees your undivided attention while you are tutoring them.
5. Listen to your tutees. Let them think and speak!
6. Establish good rapport with your tutees. Let each know that you care by showing trust, respect and acceptance.
7. Be courteous and respectful towards the tutee.
8. Build the tutee's confidence whenever possible.
9. Learn your tutee's name and pronounce it correctly.
10. Be relaxed and friendly during all sessions.
11. Make sure the tutee understands the purpose of tutoring. Important!
12. Be familiar with the vocabulary needed to converse with your "tutee."
13. Be prepared for each session. This is a key to success. Plan!
14. Be prompt and ready at the assigned times.
15. Know the skills that you are working on for each tutee each day.
16. Use correct language and pronunciation during your tutoring sessions.
17. Never let your tutees struggle with their answers to the point of frustration.
18. Let your tutees know you are human too. Don't be afraid to make mistakes or say, "I don't know."
19. Be familiar with the location of materials.
20. Keep your records accurate and up-to-date.
21. Know the classroom and the school rules and abide by them. Be a model.
22. Ask for help when you face a situation that requires assistance or a problem that you can't answer.
23. Never criticize the supervising teacher or rules of the class during the tutoring session.
24. Stay excited, enthused, and "up" for all sessions. You may be the only one that day to do that for your tutee!
25. Maintain confidentiality.

Reflection:

Imagine that all of the trust you have been given is inside a tube of toothpaste. You think, "Well, I'll let a little trust out by telling just one person about the skill level of my tutee."

Take the toothpaste and squeeze out some past. Then you realize, "Oops.... I shouldn't have violated the trust.... I'll put it back." Try to push the toothpaste back into the tube. Does it go back? NO! Because once trust or confidence is lost, it's out—it's gone. It takes a long time to build confidence and trust. It only takes that long (snap your fingers) to break it.

6.07 Reading Selection

Responsibilities Chart

Purpose:
To list responsibilities for tutor, teacher, and coordinator to insure that all parties understand assigned tasks.

Task	Tutor	Supervisory Teacher	Program Coordinator
Recordkeeping	x	monitors and oversees at all times	
Learning skill games	x		
Organizing games for a skill game day	x		
Determining (diagnosis) skills		x	
Pre-Post testing tutees for skills.		x	
Training tutors			x
Grading tutors		x	x
Preparing and administering tutor's exam		possibly	x
Providing outside assignments for tutors		x	x
Keeping folders and forms	x		
Keeping attendance	x	x	
Pre-Post test for tutors			x
Keeping materials in order for tutoring	x		
Making games—flash cards	x	directs the tutors	
Tutoring	x		
Attend in-service training	x	x	x
Discipline of tutees		x	
General management of tutees	x		
Identifying location to tutor		x	
Identifying reinforcement techniques	x	x	x

Tutoring: Learning by Helping

6.08 Skill Practice
What Should You Do If?

Purpose:

To provide practice in anticipating situations that may occur in tutoring and determine the appropriate response based on the role of the tutor.

Directions:

Answer each of the following:

What would you do if:

1. Your tutee asked to go to the bathroom or water fountain?

2. Your tutee refused to give you answers to your drill work?

3. Your tutee doesn't sit in the same seat daily?

4. Your tutee tries to talk to other students during your tutoring session?

5. Your tutee seems to be angry or upset when you first sit down to tutor?

6. Your tutee doesn't want you to tutor anymore?

7. Your tutee asks that you extend the session?

8. Your tutee asks you for a date?

9. Your tutee sits down and starts to cry?

10. Your tutee purports to be sick?

11. Your tutee won't sit close enough for you to hear the answers?

Suggestions:

You may wish to work in pairs to identify what you would do in each of these situations or develop a role play for each one. You might want to do a simulation which would include examples of each. Remember that the task is to understand your *role* as the tutor and the *responsibilities* you hold. Your responses should reflect your understanding of your role and responsibilities to others with whom you will work.

6.09 Skills Practice
First Meeting

Purpose:

To provide practice for the initial meeting in tutoring.

Directions:

You are the tutor. Your task is to meet the tutee. You will be tutoring for the first time. It is your responsibility to make the tutee feel at ease and to face the prospects of tutoring as a rewarding experience. List the things that you feel would be important to say or do on the first meeting.

Questions to Ask Yourself:

1. What would you want to know about your tutee?

2. What would you want to tell the tutee about you?

3. If the tutee asked why you wanted to be a tutor, what would you say?

4. What are the very first things you plan to say?

5. Why is the "first meeting" important?

6. What should you explain about tutoring?

7. What kind of "active listening" skills will you use?

Practice:

1. Create your own interest survey. List questions you would ask.

2. Pair with another student. Use an interest survey and go through ten minutes of a first meeting.

Elizabeth Sabrinsky Foster, Ed.D.

6.10 Reading Selection
How to Begin a Lesson

Purpose:

To provide information on "how to begin" a lesson.

Directions:

Read the following and take the 5-question test.

1. Always try to establish a warm, relaxed and pleasant atmosphere in which to work with your tutees. It is important that they feel welcome and wanted.

2. Begin each session with pleasant and friendly conversation, such as, "How is your day going so far?" "How'd you do on that math test last week?" Ask your student some question indicating concern for well being. Conversation that allows them to talk about things they like to do will produce more cooperative working relationships.

3. Make sure you are ready with the assignment materials when the student sits down.

4. Explain what the goal of the work will be for that tutoring session and what you hope to accomplish.

5. Set the timer. Begin to work.

6. Praise the student for correct answers. This is crucial! Praise is important and will be one of the most effective teaching tools you can employ. Remember the benefits of "positive reinforcement."

7. When the time is up, let the students see their grade for the day. If for some reason there is not enough time to figure it before the students go back to their classwork, then be sure to let them see it first thing the next day. Students should always be able to see their day-to-day progress and be able to evaluate their growth so that they recognize the worth of time spent in tutoring.

Test Yourself

Circle the letter in front of the correct answer.

1. At the beginning of the tutoring lesson, you:
   A. Start immediately with the work, because you know your tutee well.
   B. Ask your tutee to sit by you and begin with a little friendly conversation.
   C. Tell your tutee that from now on there will be tutoring lessons every day.

2. Your tutee comes in and sits across the room. You should:
   A. Smile and invite the student to sit beside you.
   B. Begin the tutoring anyway.
   C. Speak softly so that the student will come over to hear you.

3. After beginning with friendly conversation, you are ready to shift to a school subject. Which of these questions is the kind you should ask next?
   A. "What do you want to do now?"
   B. "What did the Astros do last night?"
   C. "How did you do in science today?"

4. Start by asking your tutee school work questions that:
   A. Were missed on the last test.
   B. You think the student should know by now.
   C. You are sure the student can answer.

5. During the conversation and the school work questions, you should take an opportunity to:
   A. Ask the student about school.
   B. Test the student's knowledge of school subjects.
   C. Praise the student.

Answers

1. B. You are establishing a relaxed, pleasant atmosphere. Not (A); no matter how well you know your tutee, you still need to set the right mood for a successful lesson. Not (C); this approach established a rigid frame rather than a relaxed atmosphere.

2. A. It's friendlier, and both of you can see the lesson. Not (B); your tutee can't see the lesson. Not (C); your tutee might not.

3. C. You are asking a question related to school work. Not (A); you aren't going to give choices. Not (B); you want to focus on the skills learned, not about a game watched the night before.

4. C. This gives you an opportunity to praise the tutee. Not (A) or (B); you want to be sure he tutee is successful at this time.

5. C. Praise makes the student feel confident and capable. Not (A); you don't' want to ask about school at every opportunity, just when it's relevant. Not (B); the student will do better feeling successful before you start to test.

6.11 Reading Selection

How to Handle Right and Wrong Answers

Purpose:

To provide information on the correct method of handling answers.

Directions:

Read the following items and discuss.

How to Handle Right Answers

Remember the following guidelines in dealing with "correct" answers.

1. Give praise and rewards at the appropriate time.
2. A right answer must be both complete and correct.
3. Praise your student after every correct answer.
4. When your student gives a right answer on the first try, without help, give special recognition.
5. If your student fishes for answers, get a commitment before you respond.
6. Let the tutee know it is all right to try even if unsure of the answer.
7. If your tutee doesn't answer, do these things:
    A. Calmly ask the question again, give a hint, ask another question that might elicit the same answer, be encouraging!
    B. Sound pleased when you get an answer, and praise the student if it's right.
    C. Don't make an issue of the resistance.

How to Handle Wrong Answers

Remember the following guidelines in dealing with incorrect answers.

1. Correct your tutee's work without being discouraging.
2. Don't say 'no" or "that's wrong" and *never* make fun of answers.
3. Always try to get a right answer before going on to the next problem.
4. If the student's answer is incomplete, help the student with the question and answer.
5. If the answer is incorrect, give clues to help discover the answer.
6. If the student appears unsure, use an appropriate wait time of 2 or 3 extra seconds. Remember that wait time can give a little extra thinking time. It may be what the tutee needs to be able to answer. In addition, the tutee knows that you are *not* going to jump in and automatically give the answers.
7. Once the student has discovered the right answer, repeat the question, have the student repeat the right answer, and provide praise.
8. Be sure the student understands what the error was and give another opportunity later to repeat the question and answer so that the correct answer is reinforced.
9. Remember *How Students Learn Best* (5.03 Reading Selection). If the tutee consistently gets the wrong answer, review the different ways you might involve the student and try another approach until you find one that provides success for the student.

6.12 Reading Selection

Structure of the Tutoring Session

Purpose:

To provide the format in which the tutoring is structured.

Directions:

Read the following and discuss:

The format of each tutoring session should be highly structured, yet flexible within the confines of the basic guidelines. What that means is, though there are some basic guidelines about seating, time, and subject format, the means of achieving stated goals are flexible and open to change as needed.

1. Each tutor is assigned up to a maximum of four students—one at a time.
2. The assigned students to be tutored remain the same throughout the year unless there is a request from either tutor or tutee for a change. (Usually considered at the semester.)
3. The tutoring session is ten minutes in length per tutee.
4. In a content subject or a skill requiring reflection and higher order thought process, the tutoring session will continue for 15 minutes.
5. Each tutor is provided with a timer to insure equal length of time per session for each student.
6. Tutoring occurs daily Monday through Thursday. Friday is a day for training (alternating with activities or learning games in the tutoring environment.)
7. Each tutor is required to keep accurate records of each session.
8. Each tutee has a folder in which all the records are maintained by the tutor.
9. The three basic record forms to be kept by the tutor include:
    A. Tally sheet
    B. Progress record
    C. Grade sheet
10. If a game day is included in the tutoring program, the tutor is required to:
    A. Select a game based on identified skill needs
    B. Organize the game
    C. Play the game with the group of tutees with a common identified skill area
    D. Record the results
11. The time at the end of tutoring sessions should be used constructively. If you can be of help to the instructor, offer to do so. Otherwise, use the extra minutes to your own benefit. Just be sure to be quiet and create no disturbances.

Sample Schedule I

	Monday	Tuesday	Wednesday	Thursday	Friday
Tutor A	Tutee 1-10 min.	Tutee 1-10 min.	Tutee 1-10 min.	Tutee 1-10 min.	Training or Skill Games (alt. weekly)
	Tutee 2-10 min.	Tutee 2-10 min.	Tutee 2-10 min.	Tutee 2-10 min.	
	Tutee 3-10 min.	Tutee 3-10 min.	Tutee 3-10 min.	Tutee 3-10 min.	
	Tutee 4-10 min.	Tutee 4-10 min.	Tutee 4-10 min.	Tutee 4-10 min.	

6.13 Reading Selection

Tutoring Procedures

Purpose:

To provide the procedures by which you will operate.

Directions:

Read the following:

1. When entering the room the tutor should:
   A. Go to the files and get out the folders for each tutee.
   B. Get one timer for the session.
   C. Go to the tutoring materials and get what is needed for the 3 or 4 sessions for that day.
   D. Make sure the area is clear of everything except tutoring material.
   E. Make sure that there is a writing instrument handy and blank paper for figuring.
   F. Begin to work after calling or going to the first student to be tutored.

2. You will have your materials ready and in hand when you begin with the tutee. This should include:
   A. Tutee folder with progress record, tally sheet, game sheet, and weekly grade sheet.
   B. Timer.
   C. Pen or pencil.
   D. Tutoring materials with which to tutor.

3. Sit down and set the timer for ten minutes. (Fifteen minutes if so instructed.)

   This ten minutes goes very quickly. You have no time to waste. It is up to you to maintain a business-like approach. Your treatment of the tutoring session as something serious lets the tutee know it is important and this will help you maintain control of the situation. Work steadily until the timer goes off.

4. You will proceed with ten minutes of drill activity as outlined by the instructor.

5. You will keep an accurate record of the number of correct and incorrect answers every day and tally those at the end of the week.

6. You will plot the progress record *daily!!!*

7. When the tutoring sessions are completed the tutor:
   A. Calculates the grade or score for each tutee if it was not done at the conclusion of each session (notify the tutee of the grade).
   B. Records all information for the day's work.
   C. Replaces the folder for each tutee in the file.
   D. Replaces the timer.
   E. Replaces the material used for tutoring in the proper place, in the proper order, quietly without disturbing other students or tutoring sessions.
   F. Sits down with a book or assignment that can be completed until time for the class to end.

Reasons for the Use of the Timer

1. Structures time for the tutors.
2. Provides psychological reinforcement for tutees in that they are continually aware of the time used and unused.
3. The number of items completed per day has little to do with the grade for the day. Do not figure on a certain number of items daily. Rather use the amount of time in the best possible way.
4. Insures equal time for each student.
5. Structures the tutoring time, thus reinforcing the intensity.
6. Provides consistent statistical data on tutoring. The structure must be uniform for each tutor.

Discussion:

In reviewing these procedures, are there any which are unclear or need further explanation?

Suggestion:

Be sure to visit the classroom(s) in which you will be working. Get familiar with the set up: where you will sit and the location of the folders and tutoring materials. Make your visit *before* you begin tutoring and take time to talk with the supervising teacher(s).

Chapter 7
Content Area Instruction Through Tutoring

Chapter Concepts:
1. Content area instruction can be supported or supplemented through tutoring.
2. Providing specific teaching techniques will strengthen your ability to tutor.

Chapter Objectives:
1. To provide you with the skills necessary to tutor in the content area assigned.
2. To provide specific practice for you to develop tutoring skills in the content area assigned.

Chapter Description:
This chapter provides information basic to many content fields. There will be practice exercises for each content area. Basic "reading" tools will be emphasized throughout the chapter as they apply in each content area.

Chapter Vocabulary:
Vocabulary for this chapter is listed at the beginning of the chapter and in subsequent areas within the chapter.

Contents

7.01	Can You Learn to Read?	Activity	79
7.02	Reading Definitions	Reading Selection	79
7.03	Teaching Sight Skills	Reading Selection	80
7.04	Worksheet for Sight Word Recognition	Reading Selection	81
7.05	Do's and Don'ts for Using Context	Reading Selection	82
7.06	Worksheet in Context Clue Usage	Skills Practice	82
7.07	Interpreting Three Levels of Comprehension	Reading Selection	83
7.08	Worksheet for Literal Comprehension	Skills Practice	84
7.09	A Five-Part Strategy for Word Attack	Reading Selection	84
7.10	Prefixes, Suffixes and Roots	Reading Selection	85
7.11	Textbook Assignment Improvement	Reading Assignment	87
7.12	SQ3R Textbook Study Skill	Reading Selection	88
7.13	Tutoring Materials: Textbook and Flashcards	Reading Selection	89
7.14	Use of Textbook Vocabulary Flashcards	Reading Selection	90
7.15	Vocabulary Slip	Activity	91
7.16	Reading Skills Related to English	Reading Selection	91
7.17	Worksheet for Sequence Ability	Skills Practice	92
7.18	Reading Skills Related to Mathematics	Reading Selection	93
7.19	Interpreting Symbols in Mathematics	Reading Selection	94
7.20	Math Vocabulary	Reading Selection	96
7.21	Newspaper Math Activities	Reading Selection	21
7.22	Reading Skills Related to Social Studies	Reading Selection	98
7.23	Student Difficulties in Reading Social Studies Materials	Reading Selection	99
7.24	Study, Comprehension, and Vocabulary Skills Pertinent to Social Studies	Reading Selection	100
7.25	Social Studies Vocabulary	Reading Selection	101
7.26	Reading Skills Related to Science	Reading Selection	102
7.27	Applying Tutoring Skills in Science to Improve Vocabulary	Reading Selection	103
7.28	Science Vocabulary	Reading Selection	104
7.29	Ways to Improve Context Clue Power in Foreign Language	Reading Selection	105
7.30	Reading Skills Related to Physical Education and Health	Reading Selection	109
7.31	Reading in Physical Education and Health Education	Reading Selection	109
7.32	Applying Tutoring Principles to the P.E. Program	Reading Selection	110
7.33	Reading Skills Related to Music	Reading Selection	111
7.34	Reading in Music	Reading Selection	112
7.35	Lesson: Basic Reading in/on Music	Skill Practice	113

Chapter 7 — Content Area Instruction Through Tutoring

7.01 Activity
Can You Learn to Read?

Purpose:

To demonstrate how difficult it is to learn to read.

Directions:

1. Read the vocabulary words.

/	=I	.(	= IS	$(!)	= HOPE
O/U/	= READ	) (	= TO	,"/(	= THAT
? ¢/	= YOU	-/(	= FUN	US.	= CAN
_ 1%	= FOR	%./,	= THIS	),/!O	= LEARN
:+"	= YES	/:	= NO	)+:/	= LIKE
0-0	= NOT	/)	= IT	?.	= WE

2. Decode the message.

?. $(!)   ,"/(%./,   .(

_____

-/C   _ 1%?   ¢/ .   / $(!)

_____

? ¢/   US.   ),/!O   ) (O/U/ .

_____

3. Make your own message and have another student decode it.

_____

_____

Follow-up:

How hard was it to read the message? Imagine that this was your experience every time you tried to read. How would you help someone who couldn't read at all?

7.02 Reading Selection
Reading Definitions

Purpose:

To provide a list of reading terms with which the student should be familiar.

1. **Visual Discrimination-Visual Perception:** to be able to see differences.
2. **Auditory Discrimination:** to be able to hear and determine sounds in words.
3. **Blending of sounds:** combinations of the sounds of 2 or 3 letters together while retaining the sounds of the individual letters, e.g. as in crayon.
4. **Initial sound:** beginning sound of a word.
5. **Medial sound:** middle sound of a word.
6. **Ending sound:** the last sound of a word.
7. **Basal reader:** reading book designed for a specific grade level, usually in elementary school.
8. **Pre-primer:** textbook covering the very basic elements of reading.
9. **Levels of reading:**

    Free reading level: Students can function adequately without teacher help.

    Instructional level: Students can function adequately with teacher guidance and yet be challenged to stimulate their reading growth.

    Frustration level: Students cannot function adequately. They often show signs of tension and discomfort.

10. **Sight vocabulary:** recognize the whole word on sight.
11. **Structural analysis:** study of the parts of a word-roots, prefixes, suffixes, and so forth.
12. **Comprehension Levels:**

    Literal: concerned with specific information.

    Interpretative: to infer or clarify.

    Critical: to judge or evaluate.

13. **Context clue:** parts of a sentence or paragraph that will help to understand unknown parts.

7.03 Reading Selection
Teaching Sight Skills

Purpose:

To provide a basic foundation for teaching sight vocabulary.

Directions:

Read the following principles and discuss.

What do we know about sight vocabulary? We know that it is acquired only after great practice and exposure to many types of reading materials. Most of us now have very large sight vocabularies. We learn through a variety of ways. Without a large sight vocabulary, the more difficult it is to read daily experience-type materials. The task of mastering a sight vocabulary, for the older student can be quite complex and arduous.

There are a number of principles that you should familiarize yourself with and consequently, upon which you should develop your tutoring techniques if you are working to help someone develop a sight vocabulary.

Principle I:

Proceed from the familiar to the unfamiliar a step at a time.

Principle II:

Move from dependence on the tutor to independence.

Principle III:

Teach the student a variety of ways of recognizing words.

Principle IV:

Introduce new words, skills, techniques, gradually and with adequate repetition so that the learner has a growing feeling of mastery.

Principle V:

Use an interesting way of having individuals practice recognizing new words.

Principle VI:

If the individual needs drill on recognition of words, try to provide it in a variety of ways.

Principle VII:

A student's knowledge of progress is extremely important.

Principle VIII:

In each lesson, try to maximize the probability of success.

Principle IX:

Consult with the student's teacher.

Principle X:

Follow a sequence for teaching word recognition.

Comment:

What does it mean when you see "variety of ways?" That means to use as many senses as you can to introduce the word:

sight — look at the word

sound — listen to the word, say the word

touch — write the word, trace the word

Show the word on cards, write it on paper, on the blackboard, on a flannel board. Make the student do the same. Have the student find the word in written context. What other varieties could you provide?

Remember:

See it!

Say it!

Write it!

Feel it!

Hear it!

7.04 Skill Practice
Worksheet for Sight Word Recognition

Purpose:
To provide practice in a lesson on sight word recognition.

Directions:
In each row, circle the word unlike the other three.

1. resentence	repentence	repercussion	resentence
2. solarium	slander	solarium	solarium
3. superstition	superstition	superstituion	supplemental
4. ultimate	ulcerous	ultimate	ultimate
5. independent	indeterminant	indeterminant	indeterminant
6. jeopardy	jeopardy	jeopardy	jealous
7. medium	medium	medley	medium
8. mildew	mileage	mildew	mildew
9. navy	naval	naval	naval
10. presumption	presumption	presumption	prevention
11. transverse	transection	transverse	transverse
12. utopia	utopia	unicorn	utopia
13. trumpet	trumpet	trumpet	trooper
14. version	verse	version	version
15. enumerate	enumerate	enumerate	enumeration

Tutoring: Learning by Helping

7.05 Reading Selection
Do's and Don'ts for Using Context

Purpose:

To provide guidelines on a technique in teaching vocabulary.

Directions:

Read the following and discuss.

DO Rely on Context Clues

1. When you have an "unmissable clue"-a direct explanation.
2. When you have highly revealing clues and the meaning you arrive at definitely "clicks" with the rest of the passage.
3. When, in view of your purpose for reading the selection, you need only a general sense of the meaning.

DON'T Rely on Context Clues
(Turn to your dictionary.)

1. When you require a precise meaning, it almost always takes the dictionary to pin the meaning down.
2. When the word is a key word, one crucial to your understanding, and full comprehension is important to you.
3. When the clues suggest several possibilities-the meaning might be one of several-and you must know which.
4. When you don't know the nearby words.
5. When you have encountered the word a number of times, realize that it is a common, useful one which you will meet again, and you will want to master it thoroughly for future reading.

Practice:

1. Identify some key words from a passage in a textbook.
2. Use a social studies or science book.
3. Once the words are identified, determine whether a context clue approach is the most effective or useful approach.

7.06 Skill Practice
Worksheet in Context Clue Usage

Directions:

Circle the word that belongs in the blank.

1. Only the outraged woman entered the hall in such a _____ way.
   trumpet   hysteric   triumph
2. The _____ snow mountain was on the verge of being a snow slide.
   terminal   treacherous   tingle
3. The uncontrolled _____ rushed to the prison to free the inmates.
   mob   myth   milieu
4. The _____ or disk mounted to spin rapidly, was the topic of discussion in science last Tuesday.
   gypsum   gunnery   gyroscope
5. Though the man had not _____ a great deal of wealth; he was not poor.
   acclimated   ascertained   accumulated
6. The authorities attempted to _____ her right of speech, but she carried on without their approval.
   suppress   suspect   supreme
7. It was a tale of sadness, _____, isolation, and unhappiness.
   loneliness   gaiety   lonesome
8. The doctor, a man of great _____, spoke to the class about cardiac surgery.
   wise   wisdom   whimsy
9. The constitution of the U.S. may seem to be _____, but it is still one of the most viable documents in use today.
   outdated   outlandish   occupied
10. _____ she isn't; she doesn't say one thing and then do another.
    Hypochondriac Hypocrite Hypodermic

Elizabeth Sabrinsky Foster, Ed.D.

7.07 Reading Selection

Interpreting Three Levels of Comprehension

Purpose:

To provide information on use of teaching comprehension skills.

Directions:

Read the following and discuss:

There are three levels of comprehension:

1. Literal
2. Interpretative
3. Critical

It is important that you understand all three levels in order to vary your types of questions that will elicit responses on all three levels and to understand the types of skills under each category.

The *literal level* is the first level. It is the level that requires the least exploration and thought on the part of the learner. The literal level involves the following skills:

1. Details
2. Specific fact finding
3. Following directions
4. Sequencing

The literal level is like reading *"on* the lines." This level usually focuses on factual information that can be recalled from memory. It does not involve deep meaning.

The *interpretative level is* the second level. It is the level that requires the reader to understand relationships. The student must be able to put things together and find answers based on assimilation. The following skills are involved on the interpretative level:

1. Cause-effect
2. Main idea
3. Inferring time, place, mood
4. Classifying
5. Inferring motives
6. Responding to imagery
7. Compare-contrast

The interpretative level is like reading *"between* the lines."

This level requires that one go beyond simply recall. It requires understanding and comprehension of the meaning of a passage.

The *critical level* is the third level. It is the most difficult and complex level. It requires that the learner draw upon all the information at hand and make evaluation type decisions. Skills involved in critical thinking:

1. Making judgments
2. Evaluating
3. Assessment
4. Determining value

The critical level is like reading *"beyond* the lines." This level requires the reader to have a thorough understanding and capacity to use thinking skills associated with analysis and judgment.

Tutoring: Learning by Helping

7.08 Skill Practice

Worksheet for Literal Comprehension

Purpose:

To provide practice in a lesson on literal comprehension.

Directions:

Read each sentence silently. Then circle the word that gives the information for the *italicized* word.

1. The *president* tells us where to go.
   when why how what who where
2. The water carried John's boat *into the channel.*
   when why how what who where
3. The girl hid as *quietly* as she could.
   when why how what who where
4. *The story* told of many different fashion styles.
   when why how what who where
5. *At sundown* my father starts to work.
   when why how what who where
6. The school released its students *very quickly* once the firm alarm went off.
   when why how what who where
7. John will give Theresa *a picture* for her birthday.
   when why how what who where
8. It was *at the movie* that the couple met.
   when why how what who where
9. *Turkey pie* is the dessert for Thanksgiving.
   when why how what who where
10. My mother is going to *Ohio* for my sister's wedding.
    when why how what who where

7.09 Reading Selection

A Five-Part Strategy for Word Attack

Purpose:

To provide a specific technique for teaching vocabulary.

Directions:

Read the following and practice:

1. Launch your attack by searching the word's context for clues.

   Crack down on the word instead of reading right on past it without a try. Context is likely to be your most important single aid. How a word is used in the sentence can often lead to its meaning.

2. Look for word part clues.

   Take the word apart if you can. Do you recognize any part? A root? A prefix? A suffix? An inflectional ending? Words that at first look difficult can often be broken down into well known building blocks. Considering the context again, do you recognize the word?

3. Work through the word, syllable by syllable. "Divide and conquer."

   Try to sound out the word by easy-to-manage syllables. Long words are just short syllables strung together. Is it familiar after all? Recalling the context, have you now solved the word?

4. Try a shift in pronunciation.

   If you have not yet arrived at a word you know, attack it again by seeing if a change-perhaps in syllable division or accent- gives you a breakthrough. Again, does the word you have worked out click with the context?

5. Reach for the dictionary.

   If after Steps 1-4 the word still defies you, you have a never failing tool. Now is the time to turn to your dictionary.

Practice:

1. Identify 5 words you can use to practice.
2. Work with a partner to practice your word attack strategy.
3. Work through all 5 words using the techniques listed.
4. Reverse roles and let your partner practice with 5 new words.

7.10 Reading Selection
Prefixes, Suffixes and Roots

Purpose:
To provide a list of content affixes and roots common to specific content areas.

Prefix, Suffix Root Meaning	English	Social Studies	Science	Mathematics	Health & P.E.	Other
ambi (both)	ambiguous	ambivalent	ambilateral		amphiarthrosis	ambiversion
anti (before)	antecedent	antebellus	anterior	antemeridiem	antenatal	antechamber
anthropo (man, mankind)	anthropo-morphism	anthropology philanthropist				misanthrope
anti (against)	antagonist antihero	antipoverty antitrust	antidote antitoxin antiseptic	antiderivative	antihistamine antacid	antifreeze antipathy
auto (self)	autobiography	autocracy	autopsy			automatic
bene (well, good)		benevolent	benign			benefactor
bi (two)	bilingual	bicentennial bipartisan	biceps biconvex biped	bilinear binomial bisect	bicuspid bifocals	bicycle biplane
biblio (book)	bibliography	bibliotherapy				bibliofilm
bio (life)	autobiography biography	biochemistry	biology			anabiosis biodegradable
cent (hundred)	centenarian	centurial	centigrade	centigram		century
cide (time)		genocide homicide	insecticide			philocide
cicum (around)	circumflex	circumnavigate	circulation	circumference		circumstance
co, con, com (with, together)	coauthor collaborate	coalition coexist	coagulate compound	coefficient correlation	compete compress	component coincide
contra (against, opposite)	contradiction	contraband	counterbalance	counterclockwise		counteract
cred (credit, to believe, trust)	credulity	accreditation				credo
dec, deci (ten)				decimal	decathlon	decade
dia (across, through)	diacritical	dialectism	diagnosis	diameter	diathermal	diabetes
epi (on, upon, over)	epigram	epidermic	epicenter epidermic	epicycle		episure
graph (to write)	biography autograph paragraph	polygraph graffiti	oceanography electrograph seismograph	graph	electroencephalograph	telegraph phonograph
inter (among)	interjection interlude	intercede interior	interpolar	interpolate	intercollegiate	intercom intermezzo

Prefix, Suffix Root Meaning	English	Social Studies	Science	Mathematics	Health & P.E.	Other
		internal	intermediary		intramural	intrinsic
		intercontinental	geology		introvert	interrupt
intra, intro (inside, within)	introduction	intrastate	intracellular	logarithm		
		introspect	intravenous			
log, logy (science of, study of)	dialectology	anthropology	biology			apology
		phonology	criminology			
		psychology	paleontology			astrology
mono (one)	monograph	monarchy	mononuclear	monomianal	mononucleosis	monotone
	monologue	monolith	monomorphic			monoplane
		nonpartisan				
non (not)	nonchalant	nonaggression	nonpolar	nonlinear	nonflammable	
	nonfiction	nonaligned	nonreactive	nonnegative		nonexistent
		nonconformist				
ped (foot)	sesquipedalian	piedmont	biped		pedometer	pedicure
		expediency	centipede			pedal
poly (much, many)	polyphonic	polygraph	polyandrous	polycentric	polyphagia	impede polyester
		polygamy	polymeric	polyhedron		
pre (before)	preconceive	preamble	preaxial			precook
	preface	predecessor			precaution	
	prefix	preside				
pro (forward)	proceed	proclaim		product		prospect
	pronoun	prohibition		protractor		procreate
	pronounce	promote		problem		produce
sub (under, below)	subject	subcommittee	subatomic	subgroup	subservient	submarine
	subplot	subterranean	subhuman	subset		subdue
	subscribe	subway				
trans (across)	intransive	transaction	transference	transformation		transient
	transitive	transcontinent	transmit	transversal		transcript
	transpose	transgress	transplant			transfer
tri (three)	trilogy	trinity	trifoliate	triangle		triad
						triplet
uni (one)	unison	unify	unicellular	uniplanar		unicorn
						unanimous

7.11 Reading Assignment
Textbook Assignment Improvement

Purpose:

To provide information to clarify textbook assignments for the tutee.

Directions:

Read the following and discuss:

Content area instructors can help to solve pupils' reading and study difficulties by giving thought to the assignment they give.

A good assignment tells the student three things:

1. *What* one is to do (content).
2. *Why* one is to do it (motivation).
3. *How* one is to do it (skills).

In connection with (1), the instructor:

A. Gives the pupils information about books and other materials they are to use.

B. Indicates approximately how much time and effort the pupils are to expend.

C. Makes very clear what the pupils are expected to produce as a result of their work.

In connection with (2), the teacher:

A. Shows the pupils how the lesson is related to the larger objectives of their ongoing work, how it connects with what has gone before.

B. Demonstrates, whenever possible, the usefulness of what they are to do. "Usefulness" here is used in a broad sense to include such matters as pleasure in reading a play or the importance of some piece of historical information to the understanding of a current problem.

In connection with *(3)*, the instructor:

A. Lets the pupils know how thoroughly they are to read or study by indicating clearly what kind of recall is expected.

1. Thorough recall-remembers everything without aid.
2. Only the main points.
3. Recall only of points connected with certain topics (reading to locate and remember relevant facts).
4. Aided recall adequate for a true-false or multiple choice quiz.
5. Recall accompanied by inference or critical thinking in order to write discussion type answers or participate in class discussion.

B. Indicates the skills the students are to use, always demonstrating when they are new or difficult by doing a part of the assignment with the pupils.

7.12 Reading Selection

SQ3R Textbook Study Skill

Purpose:

To provide a textbook study skill that tutors can utilize.

Directions:

Read the following and practice:

Steps in Textbook Study

Step 1: Survey

Look through the whole assignment. Read the headings if there are any. Read the summary if there is one. Try to get the general ideas of the content of the whole lesson. Later you can place the details into the framework which you have in mind, and the whole lesson will mean more to you.

Step 2: Question

Think of the questions which are likely to be answered in the lesson. Often the heading can be very easily turned into questions. Use them! If any heading does not tell you plainly what question is to be answered in that section, use this question: What does the author expect me to learn about (this topic) from studying this section? If there are no paragraph headings, skim the section quickly for the main ideas.

Step 3: Read

Study the lesson to find the answers to the questions, do not stop to read every word carefully; concentrate on finding the main point. You cannot remember all the facts you find, so you must look for the important ones, of which there will be only one or two for each section. Don't pick out too many. Do not try to memorize the facts at this point; just sort out the ones you need as you go along.

Study Guide. Fold or rule a sheet of large sized notebook paper lengthwise, down the middle. On the left list the topics discussed in the book. If there are paragraph headings in boldfaced type, use them. If not, list the main ideas found in the preliminary survey. Leave space between topics.

When you have finished reading a section and picking out the one or two points to remember, list on the right the key words of the ideas or facts you have decided are most important for each topic. Do not do this until after you have read a section and thought about it. This is a most vital part of your studying, and you can't tell what is important until you have read all the facts.

Step 4: Recite

Go back over the lesson immediately. Cover the right hand side of your paper and check the headings on the left. Ask yourself: "Do I remember what this section was about?" or "Can I answer this question?" If you find that you cannot, you know that you must look at the key words, or even go back to the book if necessary, in order to restudy the particular part which you did not understand or have forgotten. Step 4 is very important. Giving yourself an immediate quiz on what you have just studied is the best possible way to prevent forgetting. Practice until you can recite on the whole study guide without referring to the key words. Then practice some more. This extra practice is what really pays off.

Step 5: Review

Some time later, and also before an examination, go back to your headings and questions again and quiz yourself. Reread only those parts which you have forgotten. If you have taken Steps 1, 2, 3 and 4 faithfully, you will find that you do not have too much to restudy.

Step 6: Writing

_____

_____

_____

Practice:

1. Select a textbook which would allow the opportunity to practice the SQ3R study skill method.
2. With the textbook, work in a group of 5. Each person should select one step to teach to the group. The method would then be reviewed by the entire group.
3. Practice the use of the study skill (SQ3R) with a partner.

7.13 Reading Selection

Tutoring Materials: Textbook and Flashcards

Purpose:

To demonstrate the use of the content text and flashcards.

Directions:

Read the following and discuss:

Use of Textbook as Tutoring Material

The textbook is the basic resource for content area tutoring. Accompanying flashcards developed from the textbook can be very useful.

It is important for tutors to know the following about the text with which they will be tutoring:

1. Format of the text, i.e. headings, introductory paragraphs, form of new vocabulary, end of chapter review.
2. Use of the table of contents, index.
3. Application of SQ3R study method to the text.
4. Difficulty of vocabulary and means by which you will teach it.
5. Outline helps.
6. Paragraph organization and how to summarize.
7. Location and use of charts, graphs, diagrams.

Because the classroom teacher will probably use the text as the basic reference for teaching, it will be important for the tutor to communicate with the classroom/supervising teacher regarding expectations of students, rate of movement through chapters, testing dates and requirements. If you are to help someone else in a course you must be familiar with the text and stay with the class while tutoring.

Organization of Flashcards as Tutoring Material

Flashcards, either commercially purchased or handmade are likely to be one of the basic resource materials in tutoring, especially for English and math. Flashcards are an effective method to use for "drill" type work. They should be used for reinforcement for new vocabulary, computation skills or specific reading skills.

Organization:

1. Flashcards should be organized by skill and found on a list prepared for tutors. They can be cross-referenced.
2. All flashcard packs should have a title card on top and a direction card for the stack directly after the title card.
3. Before using a flashcard pack, be sure that you are familiar with the directions. Practice once before you use them with the tutee. It is your responsibility to know what is to be used and how it is used.
4. Problems or questions should be found on the front of the flashcard with an answer to the problem or question on the back.
5. Cards should be flashed so that the student has adequate time to see the card and answer the question.
6. The card should not be held longer than seven seconds without some assistance from the tutor. If the tutees become frustrated, they may not try to answer and refuse to work for that session. Though seven seconds sounds like a short time, count it out and try it yourself. Seven seconds, when you don't know an answer, can seem more like seven minutes.
7. When you have finished with the flashcard stack(s) for the day, be sure to replace the title card on top, followed by the directions card. If the remaining cards should be in some specific order, then replace them in that form. Rubber band the stack and replace the stack in the assigned location.

Practice:

1. Identify any text you may be using in your tutoring work.
2. Make a list of vocabulary words from a chapter that are important to the understanding of that chapter.
3. From the list, create a set of flashcards that could be used.

Tutoring: Learning by Helping

7.14 Reading Selection

Use of Textbook Vocabulary Flashcards

Purpose:

To provide specific steps in the use of textbook flashcards.

Directions:

Read the following and discuss:

Vocabulary in a textbook generally presents the biggest obstacle for most students. Therefore there should be vocabulary cards and lists prepared for all content texts involved in tutoring.

Read through the reminders and procedures. Practice this format for tutoring.

Reminders:

1. Always be prepared. Review the cards that you will be using before the tutee arrives so that you are familiar with the word, pronunciation and meaning.
2. Be sure to have the text with you during each session. This will enable you to relate the vocabulary directly to the text. Keep your study pages in the classroom.
3. Always review vocabulary from the day before. Do not start new vocabulary until previously introduced words are mastered.
4. Limit the introduction of new words to *no more* than ten. In some cases, five words may be maximum. It will depend on the students, their past exposure to the vocabulary and their ability to commit new vocabulary to memory.
5. Keep a running list of mastered words. Make sure that you will always have it available. It is a good psychological boost to look at a list of words learned in past weeks of study.
6. Underline vocabulary words in the text. The cards should correspond to the underlined words in the book. You may wish to code the flashcards by including the page number of the corresponding text where the words can be found.

Procedures:

1. Flash the card.
2. Ask students to pronounce the word. If they cannot, then:
   A. Help by trying to use the phonetic approach.
   B. Help by taking the word apart structurally.
   C. Say it yourself if you can see the pupil is getting frustrated.
   D. Ask the tutee to repeat it.
   E. Find the word in the text. (Page number should be on the card.)
   F. Either the tutee or tutor can read the sentence in which the word is found.
   G. Remember: See it, say it, write it, and feel it!

   If the student can, then proceed:
   A. Ask the students if they know the meaning of the word, if so, tell you. If not, find the word in the text, read the sentence (tutor or tutee) and help determine the meaning through *context*.
   B. Analysis approach can also be used.
   C. Ask the students to repeat the word and place it in a sentence of their own that suggests knowledge of the meaning in the context.
3. Go through all five or ten word/phrases in this manner. You can develop word games, word quizzes or activities to reinforce the retention of the words.

Application:

1. Practice the flashcard procedure with a partner.
2. Select 20-30 words that could be used for a word game. Create the game as a reinforcement tool after the words have been learned.

Elizabeth Sabrinsky Foster, Ed.D.

Chapter 7 — Content Area Instruction Through Tutoring

7.15 Activity
Vocabulary Slip

Purpose:

To provide you with a means of maintaining a vocabulary file for newly learned words.

Directions:

Fill out a 3 x 5 card for each word you would like to add to your vocabulary.

New Word: _____

Sentence or place in which you find it used:

_____

Meanings:

_____

Your example of its use:

_____

Suggestions:

1. Keep cards in an index box.
2. Put initials of student's name on cards.
3. Make flashcards.
4. Use to make puzzles.
5. Keep one box per student or keep dividers in the box to separate the students' word sets.
6. Laminate the cards for future use.

7.16 Reading Selection
Reading Skills Related to English

Purpose:

To illustrate skills necessary for success in English.

Directions:

Read the following and discuss.

Skills that the successful English student should possess include the following:

1. Find the main idea.
2. Read in sequence.
3. Pick out the details.
4. Interpret charts and tables.
5. Determine the plot, setting and character development.
6. Outline.
7. Predict outcomes.
8. Interpret figurative language.
9. Write from dictation as well as original composition.
10. Use references and library resources.
11. Use context clues to unlock word meaning.
12. Correctly analyze structure of words, sentences, paragraphs and composition as well as each part's relationship to the whole.
13. Adjust rate of reading.
14. Determine purpose for reading.

Reading for a Purpose:

Determine the purpose for reading. Is it for entertainment? Is it to retain the main ideas and concepts? Is it to recall for test material? Is it to locate specific information? Is it to provide a summary of the content? Is it to broaden your information base on the subject? Decide what your purpose is and adjust your rate and style accordingly.

Rate of Reading:

Determine how fast or slowly you should read the material in order to achieve the objective for reading. Should you scan or skim? Should you read rapidly? Should you read at an average level? Should you read very slowly and carefully. The purpose for reading will determine the speed with which you read. You may need to shift the rate of reading as the type of material changes. If the difficulty level of the vocabulary is high, then slow down to adjust.

Vocabulary:

Vocabulary in English will vary a great deal as will the variety of subjects. The background of the learner will greatly affect the student's knowledge of vocabulary. Generally, English vocabulary is not technical. Knowing how to use affix and root information will greatly increase your ability to deal with new vocabulary.

Follow-up:

1. Determine what areas of English skills you may need to review.
2. Review the prefix, suffix, and root word list (7.10).
3. Make flashcards for the different content areas. These cards can be used for enrichment as well as regular instruction.

7.17 Skill Practice

Worksheet for Sequence Ability

Purpose:

To provide practice on a lesson in determining sequence.

Directions:

Read all of the steps on this page. Then think about what you usually do on a day when you go to school. Put all of the steps in the right order. Put a number 1 in front of the thing you do first. Put a number 2 in front of the thing you do next. You should put all of the things you do in the right order. Then go back and read all of the sentences again to make sure you have put them in the right order.

____ A. I put my clothes on.

____ B. I wash my face and hands.

____ C. I leave the house for school.

____ D. I wake up.

____ E. I arrive at school.

____ F. I go to my first hour class.

____ G. I get out of bed.

____ H. I get ready for lunch.

____ I. I go to my homeroom.

____ J. I brush my teeth.

____ K. I eat my breakfast.

____ L. I eat my lunch.

Follow-up:

This is an example of a sequence activity. There are many ways to help the tutee practice sequencing events. To get the idea of what sequencing is, you can use this exercise.

7.18 Reading Selection

Reading Skills Related to Mathematics

Purpose:

To demonstrate the skills necessary for success in math.

Directions:

Read the following:

Skills that the successful math student should possess include the following:
1. Read and follow directions.
2. Determine process to use.
3. Estimate answers.
4. Interpret graphs, charts and tables.
5. Solve word and number problems.
6. Translate words visually.
7. Master cumulative computation skills.
8. Identify and define symbols.

Purpose for Reading:

Determine the purpose for reading! Is it to follow directions? (Specify purpose.) Is it to analyze a word problem that you have to solve? Is it to introduce new concepts which you must retain? Is it to review or summarize?

Rate of Reading:

Adjust your rate of reading based on the purpose. If you are reading directions, read slowly and deliberately. Reread the passage to ensure that you understand the directions. If you are reading a word problem, read carefully and slowly. Identify unfamiliar vocabulary that you may need to know in order to solve the problem. If you are reading a summary, you may pick up speed provided you understand the concepts summarized.

Vocabulary:

Math vocabulary can be like a new language if you are unfamiliar with the terms. Use your knowledge of affixes and roots to help determine meanings of new terms. You may use context clues, but if you find that technique unsuccessful, try another. Try to review new words daily. The chances of remembering new terms will be greater if you review each day instead of just once a week or before an exam.

Follow-up:

1. Look at a math textbook and identify some word problems.
2. Identify the key vocabulary words in the problems which would help to unlock meaning and assist in solving the problem.

7.19 Reading Selection

Interpreting Symbols in Mathematics

Purpose:

To provide information to use when interpreting symbols or soloing word problems in tutoring.

Directions:

Read the following and discuss:

Symbols and signs in mathematics are a type of vocabulary. They should be developed sequentially and meaningfully-usually at the time when the concept related to them is developed. You should not assume that the student knows the symbol. Whenever an example is worked by students, you should question them about the meaning and use of the symbols, clarifying as necessary. In this way, gaps in understanding or misinformation can be noted and filled in or corrected.

Analyzing Statistical Reports Tables, Formulas, Equations

This material is often tabular and may include statistical equations and formulas. If the concepts represented in the material are understood, the following steps, engaged in by teacher and student together, can aid in understanding:

1. Read and understand the statement that tells what the table represents.
2. Study each vertical column of items and read the headings for them to see what they represent.
3. Study the vertical columns thoroughly to compare and/or draw conclusions.

In order to deal with formulas and equations, the student must acquire the concept that each formula and equation is a sentence in mathematical shorthand. In fact, some textbooks call equations Algebraic sentences. Therefore, a first step might be to have the student write the formula and equation in a sentence (or state it orally in class). It represents a sentence with a subject and a predicate. The operational symbols ($+$, $=$, $-$, $\bullet$, and $\times$) represent verbs. Next have the student retranslate the formula or equation into mathematical symbols.

If the formula is given in a sentence in the text, as in word problems, have the student start by translating it into its mathematical equivalent. The following formula was written in a textbook.

The square of the sum $(a+b)^2$ of two numbers $(=)$ (verb).

The square of the first number $(a)^2$ (structured word plus twice the product $2(ab)$ plus $(+)$ (structured word) the square of the second number (b^2).

Algebraic form: $(a+b)^2 = a^2 + 2ab + b^2$.

In such intensive, detailed reading, you can help your students by analyzing written version of the formula as shown, indicating to the students the basic parts of the sentence and the function of the process and structure words. Then, have them determine all known number values for the letters. At this point the students are ready to solve the formula or equation mathematically.

Solving Word Problems

The students' grasp of the concepts and their understanding of the way they should read mathematics becomes apparent as they read written problems. A specific series of steps are necessary as a guide to the students' reasoning and purposeful reading of the problem. They are:

1. Read it slowly and carefully. Picture the scene of the problem in your mind.
2. Reread the last sentence. Determine what is asked.
3. Reread the entire problem. Determine the facts given to work with.
4. Decide the process to use.
5. Estimate the answer. Judge reasonableness of estimate.

For example, these steps would be followed for the following problem:

Mr. Stone bought a new sewing machine for his wife. The store asked him to make a down payment of 20%. If the cost of the machine was $160.00, how much was the down payment?

Elizabeth Sabrinsky Foster, Ed.D.

1. The situation: Mr. Stone is buying his wife a sewing machine and he must make a specified down payment.
2. What is asked: How much is the down payment?
3. Facts given: The sewing machine cost $160.00. Down payment must be 20%.
4. Process: Multiplication to compute the size of the down payment.
5. Estimate: A little more than $30.00.
6. Compute the problem: 20% of $160.00.

Some suggestions for overseeing difficulties in reading problems are:

1. Have exercises in vocabulary study.
    A. Find meanings.
    B. Match words with objects.
    C. Grouping words that relate to the same process, i.e. plus, sum, and longer than relate to addition.
    D. Classifying and identifying words and concepts, i.e. radius, diameter, circumference, arc refer to circle.
2. Determine unfamiliar word(s) or expression(s) in a problem.
3. Begin with an easy problem and state what the numbers in the problem stand for.
4. Help the tutee to visualize the problem situation. Describe the situation presented in the problem without using the quantities cited.
5. Have the tutee read many different types of problems, i.e:
    A. One step problems: If 18 inches of ribbon are needed to tie one diploma, how many inches will be needed to tie all the diplomas for a graduating class of 106?
    B. Two step problems: Martin's Department Store was having a 98 cents sale. Danny's mother bought three tee shirts at 98 cents each, five pairs of socks at 98 cents a pair, and six towels at 98 cents each. How much did she spend altogether (not including tax)?
    C. Problems with hidden questions: A telephone pole 57 feet long fell straight across a road. If $2^{1}/_{3}$ feet were on the other side of the road, how wide was the road? Hidden question. How many feet of the pole were not on the road? (A two step problem.)
    D. Problems without numbers: What unit of measure would you use to measure the area of this page in your book? The area of New York City? The area of your classroom floor?
    E. Problems with irrelevant facts: Tim liked to sit at the street corner and count cars. During a half hour period 38 station wagons, 97 sedans, 18 convertibles, and 46 sports cars passed by. How many cars were there in all? (A one step problem.)

Practice:
1. Pair up with another tutor and work through problems A - E.
2. Make a list of concrete objects or manipulatives that you could use to help solve word problems. Look at the listed problems as starters.
3. Make a list of available manipulatives that would have access to use.

Tutoring: Learning by Helping

7.20 Reading Selection

Math Vocabulary

Purpose:

To provide a basic vocabulary necessary to understanding basic math.

Directions:

After reviewing the following list, circle the words that are new or unknown to you. Make flashcards with those words with the meaning on one side and the vocabulary on the other. Pair up with another tutor to practice learning the new vocabulary meaning.

1. **Least common denominator:** for any set of given fractions, the least common denominator (LCD) is the smallest natural number divisible by the denominators
2. **Concepts:** general ideas or understandings
3. **Parentheses:** a mark used to enclose part of the problem to be treated as an entity
4. **Computation:** to find an answer by
5. **Denominator:** in a fraction, the number below the line which states the whole number or parts of the whole
6. **Numerator:** in a fraction, the number above the line; part of the whole
7. **Equation:** linear array of a math problem separated to the left and right by an equal sign
8. **Digits:** the symbols for the numbers 0–9
9. **Negative number:** numbers less than zero
10. **Dividend:** when a number is divided, we call this number the dividend
11. **Divisor:** the number we are dividing by
12. **Quotient:** the answer in a division problem
13. **Measurement:** determining size, length, weight
14. **Geometry:** mathematical study of relationships of points, lines, angels, surfaces and solids
15. **Compare:** to examine to see similarity or difference
16. **Sum:** the result when you add numbers
17. **Addend:** a set of numbers to be added
18. **Minuend:** the number from which we subtract
19. **Subtrahend:** the number we subtract
20. **Graphs** (types: pie, bar, picture, to depict number visually
21. **Parallel:** being an equal distance apart at every part
22. **Decimal:** a number written in base ten, fractional part of 100
23. **Place value:** value of a digit in a number
24. **Estimate:** a judgment of an approximate answer
25. **Exponent:** number placed to the right and above another number which states the power
26. **Area:** measurement of surface
27. **Perimeter:** outside, or distance around
28. **Diameter:** distance across the center of the perimeter
29. **Radius:** distance from the center of a circle to the perimeter
30. **Positive numbers:** numbers greater than zero
31. **Number line:** a set of points spaced at uniform distance along a line
32. **Integer:** the whole numbers and their additive inverse 5, 4, 3
33. **Prime number:** a prime number is any number that can only be divided by itself and 1

7.21 Reading Selection
Newspaper Math Activities

Purpose:

To provide practical ideas for applying math principles.

Directions:

1. Students find pictures of people, buildings, and so forth and write the number of objects on the back of the picture.
2. Students measure the length and width of a newspaper page. They can also count the number of columns across a page, the number of articles on a page, the number of words or letters in a headline, and so forth.
3. Students study a full page grocery ad. Give them a number and have them circle it when it appears on a page. Have them count the number of times the number is used.
4. From one page of the newspaper, have the students circle words with a certain number of letters, or circle headlines with a certain number of letters, or circle headlines with a certain number of words.
5. Mount numerous headlines on index cards. Have the students play a game by drawing the cards.. The student that has the most words in his headline wins.
6. Cut the want ads into sections and distribute them to the students. Have them count the number of ads in their section.
7. Have the students go on an imaginary shopping trip by using the paper. If they had $25.00 to spend, what would/could they buy? What would they buy as a special gift for someone?
8. Have students check the birth announcements in the newspaper. Have them develop one chart of the number of boy and girl babies born. They could do the same thing with obituaries.
9. Have students read the weather reports for a specified period of time and compute the high, low and average temperatures for the period. Do the same thing with different cities.
10. Have students compare the cost of the same food items as priced in the grocery ads by different stores.
11. Have students determine what grocery items they could buy with $5.00. Have students compare their lists.
12. Develop a bingo game in which temperatures are used from a weather map. Read a temperature and have students circle it if its on their list.
13. Given the proper information from the Sports section, have students compute batting averages, won-loss %, passing averages, free throw %.
14. Have students trace or identify different geometrical shapes found in the newspaper.
15. Using full page grocery ads, have students determine the price per pound or ounce for food items. Determine what is least expensive, most expensive. Have them chart their results.
16. Have students collect articles that make reference to the metric system. Have students convert measurements in the paper to the metric system.
17. Give students a certain amount of money to take a shopping trip through the classified ads. If each student had $2,600.00 to buy a used car, what car advertised in the classifieds would they buy?
18. Have students find recipes in the paper. Double and triple the ingredients specified.
19. Have students figure the high, low, and average cost of owning or renting a home by reading the classified ads.
20. Have students compute interest rates from different business ads that include this information.
21. Have students locate the prices of houses in different sections of town by using a city map and a copy of the newspaper.
22. Have students figure the sales tax on certain items included in the paper.
23. Have students construct bar graphs of their favorite team's win-loss record, scoring average, and so forth.
24. Have students examine the stock market report for two days and identify the stocks that gained or decreased in value, and those that remained unchanged. Use companies of particular importance in your area, if possible.
25. Have students select a stock and convert the high, low, and last price into dollars and cents.
26. Have students collect math terms used in the newspaper and/or articles related to math.
27. Have students collect and identify different types of graphs used in the paper. They could construct their own graph to support an article they have read.

28. Have students determine how much they would save on certain items by examining the regular and sales prices on certain items. What percent was saved?
29. Have students develop line graphs using temperatures, and so forth reported in weather summaries.
30. Have students clip and mount pictures of new cards (or other items) that are in the same price range.
31. Have students determine increases in prices (percentages, and so forth) by comparing items advertised in today's paper with past papers.
32. Have students read travel ads and compute the cost per mile for a trip, or the distances between cities, etc.
33. Have students find the cost of a classified ad by the number of lines.
34. Use the help wanted ads to have students figure the salary range and average salary of certain jobs advertised in the paper.
35. Use any statistics found in the paper (traumatic deaths, divorces, crime rate, and so forth) to make math problems more "real" for students.
36. Have students keep track of people, places, and events in the news. After a certain period of time, have them draw a chart or graph of those that are mentioned more frequently.

Suggestion:

Make examples of some of the activities to share with your tutees. Have your folders stored in a common place. If every tutor completed two activities, the group would have the whole list for examples.

7.22 Reading Selection

Reading Skills Related to Social Studies

Purpose:

To demonstrate skills necessary for success in social studies.

Directions:

Read the following and discuss.

Skills the successful social studies student should possess include the following:
1. Find the main ideas.
2. Locate and recall details.
3. Base opinion on information.
4. Draw conclusions.
5. Determine cause and effect relationships.
6. Determine fact or opinion statements.
7. Make comparisons and contrasts.
8. Outline.
9. Use multiple references and resources.
10. Interpret maps and graphs.
11. Adjust reading speed.
12. Identify propaganda.
13. Determine sequence of events.

Reading for a Purpose:

Determine the purpose for reading. Is it to find main ideas and remember them? Is it to preview a selection? Is it to locate specific details? Is it to organize a sequence of dates or events? Is it to determine cause or effect, fact or opinion, comparison or contrast? Is it to review or summarize?

Rate of Reading:

Determine how quickly or slowly you should read the material in order to achieve the objective for reading. A preview reading would probably dictate a light, fairly quick reading. When reading for content and recall, read more closely and slowly. When looking for details, use the scan method. When identifying new vocabulary, read carefully and deliberately.

Vocabulary:

Social Studies Vocabulary, see Reading 7.25.

Follow-up:

Look at the 13 identified skills and determine whether those skills fall under literal, interpretive, or critical skills.

7.23 Reading Selection

Student Difficulties in Reading Social Studies Materials

Purpose:

To provide information on "why" students have difficulty in social studies.

Directions:

Read the following and discuss:

Social studies material is often difficult for the students to read with understanding. Much of the reason for this is the student's lack of background and actual experience with social studies information and concepts.

Textbooks in the social studies area provide a barrier to the student. Much of the student's reading instruction through the years has been based on readers, which are comprised of story-type reading material. With social studies the student is faced with factual prose jammed with data. Marksheffel states:

Most textbooks are excellent sources of information, facts, and ideas pertinent to learning in specific content areas. The material is usually of the highest caliber because it is written by experts in the particular area of concentration. The fact that textbook re written by experts is at once both a major weakness a' d a major strength. Specialists in subject matter are usually amateurs at writing. They understand so well the materials about which they write that they appear to forget that the student has but a meager knowledge of the vocabulary and concepts necessary for understanding.

Other difficulties attributed to social studies materials are:

1. Contractions of subject matter in which many facts and ideas are condensed, thereby omitting much of the concrete factual and anecdotal material that would both make the subject more alive and provide the bases for the student to relate the ideas to his own background.

2. Difficult ideas which are largely removed from the experience of the students. This problem is often compounded with the condensation of the subject matter.

3. Sentence length adds to difficulty in that complex ideas often seem to compel complex sentences. Involved sentences add to the student's difficulty with the organization and treatment of ideas. Though many textbook authors have striven to simplify the language, complex writing still persists.

4. Organization may elude students in that they may find it difficult to note the sequential development of ideas, cause and effect relationships and relevant or irrelevant data.

5. Vocabulary is a basic difficulty. The words used are either general words used in a social studies content or technical words pertinent to social studies. The student may know the meaning of the general words, but may not the social studies: for instance, storm, grant, revolution. Then there are the specialized social studies terms such as federalism, treaty, and capital, abstract terms which represent whole concepts.

6. The student may lack the skills necessary for thinking about and using the ideas within the subject. Obviously these difficulties, experienced by many students, require direct assistance through instruction by the teacher.

Follow-up:

1. Look carefully at each identified difficulty.

2. Working with a partner, identify what you would do in each case if your tutee was having any of the difficulties listed in items 1 - 6.

3. Compare your strategies with others and add to your list from the suggestions of others.

7.24 Reading Selection
Study, Comprehension, and Vocabulary Skills Pertinent to Social Studies

Purpose:

To provide information on which to base study, comprehension, and vocabulary skills approaches.

Directions:

Read the following and discuss:

The study skills are those which enable the student to attack a reading assignment in accordance with a stated purpose, to locate information, and to determine the structure of thought of the author. Obviously, the social studies teacher gives guidance and instruction when needed.

These specific principles of teaching will help the student become effective in the use of study skills:

1. Use material in the students instructional materials (textbooks) when teaching the study skills. These skills are best developed as they apply to the instructional material in class. Direct application should be made to the specific paragraph, chapter, graph, picture, etc. which is needed for clearer understanding of the subject information.

2. Be cognizant of sequence in the study skills. If the students seem to have difficulty with getting the main idea of a paragraph in which it is only implied, you will probably need to return to a simpler structure such as determining the main idea of a paragraph in which it is stated. Then, through discussion of various clues develop the skill to the implied main idea paragraph.

3. Teach the skill when the need for it arises. This practice usually brings about the best results. Motivation is highest when the students see the direct application of their learning.

4. Fuse the teaching of the skills with the teaching of content. This principle is really an extension of the first. The essential point for you is that greater competence in the skill should bring about greater mastery of the content. The content is the body of information through which the skill is taught.

Things to Do in Developing Social Studies Vocabulary

1. Write new words on the blackboard. During a discussion time, quickly review the syllabication of the word, its root, and various forms of it. If the word is democracy, note the two Greek roots and the meanings of each (demos people); (Kratein to rule) and the forms: democratic, democrat, democratization, and so forth.

2. Students list and identify names, places, and events related to the word to add to the richness of its conceptual base.

3. Suggest that the students list the words peculiar to a period of history such as whig, feudalism.

4. Have the students evaluate the definition of some figure of speech, slogan, or expression. Note the significance and the impact. For instance: What did Thomas Paine mean in the statement, "These are the times that try men's souls?"

5. Use films, recordings, tapes, drawings, dramatizations, models, and exhibits to add to the conceptual background of the words whenever possible.

6. Students note the emotional use of words. Suggest that the students use other less emotional words and notice the difference in the impact of a selection.

Practice:

1. Work in dyads or triads.

2. Identify one strategy per pair or group. Practice one of the six listed strategies.

3. Allow time for each pair or group to demonstrate how they would use the identified strategies to lead study, comprehension, or vocabulary skills.

Chapter 7 — Content Area Instruction Through Tutoring

7.25 Reading Selection
Social Studies Vocabulary

Purpose:
To learn social studies terms.

affluence	polls	minimum wage	legislation
alienation	preamble	founded	compliance
allegiance	prestige	affiliate	accomplish
aristocrat	radical	boycott	violated
artifact	rebate	insured	litigation
bureau	republican	policy	prohibit
compromise	resolution	premium	discrimination
contraband	revenue	lapse	bail
corruption	sanctions	contingent	arraignment
crusade	secession	outlet	evidence
delegate	sociology	atmosphere	waive
despotism	statue	potash	felony
diplomacy	township	refined	immunity
domestic	trade union	silt	testify
espionage	treason	Mesopotamia	witness
extradition	ultimatum	Tigris and Euphrates	reserved
federal	unanimous	geographical	jeopardize
filibuster	urban	factor	secede
fraus	veto	combine	equality
fugitive	efficiently	equator	denied
guerrilla	profit	altitude	abridged
heretic	prosperity	proposed	appropriate
humanism	coordination	recreation	provisions
inauguration	duplication	ecological	article
intolerance	capitalist	preserves	proposed
issue	production	barren	legislature
jeopardy	raw materials	tundra	ratify
lineage	consumer	access	fundamental
lobbying	intersection	preservation	differentiate
metropolis	network	executive	exempt
militia	coastal	cabinet	privacy
munitions	freight	amendment	opportunity
opponent	circulation	Constitution	custom
oppression	regulation	forbid	chamber
panic	mechanized	jurisdiction	influence
persecution	migrant	unconstitutional	favorable
petition	dependence	civil rights	representative
policy	substandard	enforcing	diversity

7.26 Reading Selection
Reading Skills Related to Science

Purpose:

To demonstrate the skills necessary for success in science.

Directions:

Read the following:

Skills that the successful science student must possess include the following:
1. Read and follow directions.
2. Interpret graphs, diagrams, charts and tables.
3. Visualize.
4. Determine sequence and follow steps.
5. Change rate of reading.
6. Select, locate and use multiple resources.
7. Identify, define and use symbols and formulas.
8. Estimate and evaluate.
9. Use scientific vocabulary.
10. Use problem solving techniques.
    A. Formulate hypothesis.
    B. Collect data.
    C. Organize data.
    D. Form conclusion.
    E. Test conclusion.

Purpose for Reading:

Determine the purpose for reading. Is it to follow directions in an experiment? Is it to analyze results from an experiment? Is it to introduce a new chapter or concept? Is it to review or summarize? Is it to define new vocabulary? Is it to interpret a diagram or table?

Rate of Reading:

Adjust your rate of reading based on the purpose. If you are reading directions, read slowly and deliberately. Reread the passage to ensure that you understand the directions. If you are reading steps to follow in an experiment or investigation, read carefully and slowly. Reread to insure proper sequence and follow up. If you are reading new material or about a new concept, first identify and define unfamiliar vocabulary read carefully and specifically for recall. Reread and review in the same day. If you are reading a summary, you may pick up speed, provided you understand the concepts and information summarized.

Vocabulary:

Scientific vocabulary is highly technical and can be like a new language if you are unfamiliar with the terms. Use your knowledge of affixes and roots to help determine the meanings of new terms. Review new words daily. The chances of remembering new terms will be greater if you review each day, instead of just once a week or before an exam.

7.27 Reading Selection
Applying Tutoring Skills in Science to Improve Vocabulary

Purpose:

To provide techniques to teach science vocabulary.

Directions:

Read the following and discuss:

The tutor can enlarge the student's vocabulary in many ways by a conscious and systematic approach.

A. Be a pace setter and show enthusiasm for the correct use of words. Develop a large vocabulary and use it in the classroom.

B. Search for ways to minimize differences between specialized words and those in every day speech. When appropriate, a common term may be used as a translation or substitution for the technical term. The main thing is to help students learn the specialized term by relating it to their experimental background.

For instance, the meaning of density in physical science is the mass per unit volume. In lay terms the words body and thickness may be used to give clues to the term. In another instance, for the term equilibrium which in one meaning is a condition in which two equal and opposing forces are operating in the same system, you can use balance. Fascinating vocabulary lessons can be taught quite spontaneously by comparing the looseness of the every day terms with the precise scientific meanings. Such a device may well relate the scientific terms to the student.

C. The complete understanding of a concept or phenomenon should be taught before citing the words that label it. Isaac Asimov's *Words of Science* does an excellent job of discussing the concept of each word presented.

D. Students should be guided to use the new words consistently in discussion and in writing.

E. Analyze the words. Note acronyms (such as laser light amplification by simulated emission of radiation). Help the students to understand how many scientific words are directly related to roots that a long word usually consists of strung together word parts, each of which has a meaning, and that the putting together of the parts usually gives the meaning of the complete word. For example, the word isotherm consists of the prefix iso, meaning equal, and the root therm, meaning heat cycloid consists of the root cycl, meaning circle, and the suffix oil, meaning that which resembles; chlorophyll consists of the root chloro, meaning green, and the root phyll, meaning leaf.

F. Strive for precision by encouraging students to say exactly what they mean. For example, would they be able to distinguish the meanings among the words spherical, globular, round?

G. Alert students to structure words which indicate the relationship between facts and ideas. Such structure words may indicate time order (after, before, while, during), cause and effect (since, because, for that reason, therefore), likenesses and differences (unlike, different, same, and comparative and superlative forms), and order of importune (least, most essential).

H. Alert the student to multiple meanings, for instance, cell as used in biology and in electricity.

I. Classify words listed at the end of a chapter or unit in accordance with the interrelationships of the concepts they represent. For instance in a chapter of a science text entitled "The Atmosphere," the vocabulary listing at the end is presented alphabetically:

atmosphere	hydrosphere	stratosphere
barometer	ionosphere	temperate zones
climate	marine climate	transpiration
conduction	mesosphere	tropics
convection	nitrogen	troposphere

Classification is a means by which you can outline main ideas determine topics and subtopics or create topical outlines.

J. Other specific suggestions for students are:

1. Note whether the new meaning is suggested by the content of the sentence or its appearance.

2. Note whether there are any pictures, diagrams, charts which may illustrate the meaning.

Tutoring: Learning by Helping

3. Note italicized words or words in boldface print (usually new technical words) and determine the meaning as given in the textbook.
4. Keep a list of new words in a notebook, each with its definition.

Understanding and Using Formulas

Formulas and the symbols used in them may be considered an extension of vocabulary, as they represent ideas by a symbolic code which can also be labeled by words. Often, the words are learned first. We may say that if words are subtractions of concepts, then formulas and specific symbols pertinent to a field are abstractions of abstractions.

A specific symbol may be represented by a word alone. However, the formula is a type of shorthand that represents a thought. In language, the sentence carries the thought. Formulas are types of sentences. If the student understands the thought and the concepts contributing to it, the only additional skill needed is translation. Perhaps the formula can be presented as a type of language with its own vocabulary. For example, the formula for computing the size of a centripetal force is:

$$F = \frac{MV^2}{R}$$

(Vocabulary)

F = force measured in newtons, dynes, pounds

M = mass measured in kilograms

V = velocity measured in minutes per second or feet per second

R = radius of the curve measured in millimeters

Expressed as a sentence the formula reads: "Centripetal force is equal to the mass times the velocity squared divided by the radius of the circle."

Try to assist the student with the interpretation of formulas. Treat all symbols and components of formulas as new vocabulary. Be sure the student recognizes, understands and can explain the meaning of the symbol or formula.

7.28 Reading Selection
Science Vocabulary

Purpose:
To provide a list of common science terms.

disease	comet	radioactive
ingredients	conductivity	reaction
inspect	constellation	radioactive
label	contaminate	reaction
nourish	corona	residue
preserve	corrosion	saline
product	crucible	saturation
protect	crystallization	seismograph
spoiling	disinfection	smog
discovery	ductile	spectroscope
illness	ecology	splashdown
humanity	effervescent	supersonic
instrument	emulsion	tenacious
method	equilibrium	uranium
germ	fallout	viscosity
organ	filtration	action
centrifuge	radioactive	atom
pioneer	sensory neuron	block and tackle
process	fluid	chemical change
machine	galaxy	control
experiment	genetics	diffusion
regulate	hydrosphere	egg cell
care	inertia	energy
cell	inorganic	fixed pulley
stomach	ionize	fulcrum
microscope	isotherm	graft
biology	isotope	hydra
discover	kinetic	instinct
affinity	malleable	level
amorphous	metallurgy	microphone
assumption	methane	mutant
astronautics	neutron	nerve impulse
binary	opaque	orbit
biodegradable	pesticide	pistil
buoyancy	phosphorescent	potential energy
chlorination	precipitate	reservoir
coagulate	quasar	telescope

7.29 Reading Selection
Ways to Improve Context Clue Power in Foreign Language

Purpose:

To provide skills on using context clues in foreign language.

Directions:

Read the following and discuss:

Teachers often observe that foreign language students need to strengthen their context clue power. Students are so worried about missing little words, they miss the larger thought. They exhaust themselves looking up each word they don't know. Then they slight the job of comprehending because their time and energy are gone.

Just how can students make the context reveal more about a new word's meaning? What specific types of context clues will they find? What kind of practice work is likely to be to their advantage?

You may feel as if you're confronted with a "new word explosion" as you first leaf through the pages of a foreign language textbook. Clearly you'll be spending a good many hours with vocabulary in the course of a year's work in a foreign language.

How can you learn the maximum amount possible from every moment you spend in vocabulary study? With what procedures should you react when you encounter an unfamiliar word? Under what circumstances? In what order? What techniques have proved effective with language students in helping them cope with heavy loads of vocabulary? How can these techniques get going for you in foreign language study?

Here are a few vocabulary tips at your fingertips. You can take advantage of them to pack sixty seconds of faster, firmer learning into every minute of study.

Tip 1: Does the context clue you in on the new word's meaning?

A university expert on reading in a foreign language had this advice for students: "The following method is guaranteed to waste a maximum amount of time and to produce minimum results. Start off with the first word of the assignment, read along until you come to a word you don't know, look that up in the vocabulary, and so forth, ad nauseam."

"A cardinal rule to follow is this: Never look up a word in the vocabulary until you have read the immediate context in which it occurs …."

A Vital Skill for YOU

Indeed, context suggests the meaning so often that one of the most vital skills for you to acquire is the use of context revelation. Whenever a new word confronts you, search the context to detect clues to its meaning. As you do so, you may develop a psychological set toward the word -you may "lay the first layer cents of cement for fixing the term in your vocabulary."

How far beyond the word should you read? The university expert continued: "It would be idiotic to look up a word before reading through the whole sentence in which it occurs." In some cases you may want to read through the whole paragraph or beyond.

A Flash Revelation

As you read on, you may suddenly have a flash revelation of the meaning. You may encounter the puzzling word in another setting—this one rich in added clues. You may come across a photograph or drawing with details that illuminate the meaning. Of course, illustrations are part of a word's environment and often reward you with clues.

Perhaps, at your first encounter with the word, you found yourself deliberating over two or three possible meanings. As you discover further clues, you may find you can now commit yourself to one particular meaning.

Among your vocabulary competencies should be sharp powers of clue detection. You'll make a conscious, deliberate attack on the context to wrestle from it all it will reveal of the new word's meaning. In class your teacher will probably alert you to some of the context clues that abound to help you in your reading.

When you first practice exploring context, you will want to check your tentative meanings immediately by consulting the vocabulary section of your foreign language dictionary. Later, the decision when to and when not to look up a word will be guided by the do's and don'ts of using context, to be suggested later.

Tip 2: Does the word or group of words look like some word or expression you already know?

New words that are related to well known English words should yield their meaning quickly. They do so because they have an ancestor in common with the English word, resemble it, and have the same or a similar meaning. Such words are called "cognates."

A Family Resemblance

Like members of a family, all the "relatives" below look alike. They all mean captain:

capitaine in French

capitan in Spanish

Kapitan in German

capitano in Italian

capitaneus in Latin

Luckily, you'll find cognates at every turn in languages that have become interrelated in their historical development. You'll want to make the most of these look alikes.

Deceivers

Will the use of cognates ever lead you astray? Some cognates, indeed, are deceivers. In French and Spanish, the words actual and actual look easy. But, surprisingly, they mean "existing right now," "immediate," not the so obvious "actual" or "real" or "genuine." Pain in French means "bread" and dispense me in Spanish means "excuse me," not "dispense with me!"

Yes, there are notorious false cognates. Some of these you'll recognize because their meanings fail to click with the context. Others your teacher will call to your attention. Fortunately, there are relatively few false cognates. The large numbers of true cognates contribute greatly to the effectiveness of intelligent guessing.

Tip 3: Can you discover a clue in a familiar part?

Take the word apart if you can. Do you recognize any part a prefix, a root, a suffix? Guess all you can from any part you recognize. When you do discover a part you know, your gain is usually great.

In French, Spanish, German, and Italian, the following prefixes help you "unlock" numbers of words:

con- together, with

*inter-*between

*inter-*between

*pan-*all

*re-*again

*trans-*across

In all four of these languages, the following roots help you reason out the meaning of a far flung family of related words:

*dic-*say

*audi-*hear

*graph-*writing, record

*scrib-*write

*voc-*call

Though it is not often possible to get at the precise meaning of a word through its component parts, a part you recognize helps you remember the meaning once you've ascertained it. It's a handle to take hold of in retention.

Is there a preferred sequence for exploring the new word's context, giving thought to cognates, analyzing word parts? Not really! Actually, you may get a notion from any one of these test it then discard, modify, or confirm it.

Tip 4: If tips 1, 2, and 3 haven't yielded all the meaning you want, turn to the vocabulary section or reach for your foreign language dictionary.

If you require a more precise meaning of it or if your tentative meaning needs verifying, now is the time to look the new word up. The timing gives you full benefit of the mental set you developed by trying to deduce the meaning.

You may be wondering, "Just when should I rely on context, and when should I look the word up?" Here in a capsule are a few do's and don'ts:

Do rely on clues from context, cognates and word parts:

1. When you have highly revealing clues and when the meaning you arrive at definitely clicks with the rest of the passage.
2. When, in view of your purpose in reading the selection, you need only the approximate meaning.

Don't rely on clues look the word up:

1. When the word is a key word, crucial to your understanding and full comprehension is important to you.
2. When you require a precise meaning. It usually takes the dictionary to pin the meaning down.
3. When the clues suggest several possibilities, the meaning might be any one of several and you don't know which.
4. When you don't know the nearby words.
5. When you have encountered a word a number of times, you realize that it is one you will meet again, and you want to master it thoroughly for future reading.

Tip 5: If the word is an important one for you to retain, you may wish to record it (on a divided page in a notebook or on flashcards) for future study.

Students say, "I've looked that word up four times, and I still can't remember it!" You can put words on instant call through powerful techniques for retention. Which words are you likely to want to record to work on further?

Word or Idiom Meaning
Illustrative Sentences (Optional)

Test your understanding by covering answers.

1. By the time a word has blocked you three times, chances are it will block you many times more. If you own your book, you might make a dot in the vocabulary section beside a word each time you look it up then record for special study words that have three dots.

2. You may want to record deceptive cognates, but you probably won't need to record words with exact or almost exact correspondents in English.
3. You will very likely wish to record your "error demons" words whose meanings persistently elude you.
4. Troublesome idioms should be recorded.
5. Your teacher will stress words you'll run across often.
6. Authors of textbooks often spotlight words they consider essential through the vocabulary lists that accompany each lesson.

How to Make and Use a Divided Page

Rule off a sheet of notebook paper vertically into three columns. Enter the word or idiom in the first column; the particular meaning in the center column; and original illustrative sentences (if you wish to include these) in the third column.

Now turn on the "most powerful study technique known to psychologists": self-recitation. Conceal the meaning column with your hand or with an index card used as a cover card, and try to express the meaning. Then lift the card and check. Keep checking until you have full mastery.

Vocabulary Term or Idiom

Print here: _____

Write the meaning here:

_____

Write brief illustrative sentences (optional) below:

_____
_____
_____

Or operate the other way. Expose the meaning column, conceal the new word column, and see if you can supply the new word. Mark items that are still "error demons" and double check these next time.

How not to learn vocabulary is to read and reread dutifully (and all too often dreamingly) a list of new words and their definitions. How to learn vocabulary is to spend much of your study time (perhaps as much as four fifths) in self-recitation. The cover card forces concentration as you struggle to recall what's underneath. You can fold your "current" pages carry it around with you, and work on it during odd moments.

How to Use Flashcards

You may prefer standard 3 x 5 index cards for your word collection. Record the word or idiom by itself on one side of the card and the meaning on the reverse side. Look at the word, then ask yourself the meaning. Or check yourself the other way work from the meanings to the new word.

Flashcards offer several advantages over the divided page: (1) As you study, you can separate your cards, with rubber bands, into an "I do know" pile and an "I don't know" pile. (2) You can "retire" words that you feel have become permanently yours, replace these with new ones, and free yourself to concentrate on current problem words.

You may be thinking, "That's a lot of work and time and bother!" Of course, recording a word takes time probably, for each entry, three or four minutes of your too crowded day. But you'll actually be making entries for relatively few words. Mastery of many words will come about naturally as you go over a lesson, meet them in reading, or hear them in class. Thus, there is no necessity for recording most of the new words you'll meet.

Then, too, the very act of entering a word will help you remember the word. If you were to do no more than make the entry, then lose your word collection never to find it again, you would still be ahead. The mere motor act of writing, in and of itself, would have strengthened your learning.

How to Make a Word Entry

Would you like a clincher for retention? If so, you might add to your divided page (third column) or to your flashcard (meaning of) three short sentences of your own in which you use the word. Takes too much time? Chances are you'll regain the time through firmer learning. And you should collect an important fringe benefit in the ease with which the new word now slides into your own speaking and writing.

See It! Say It! Hear It! Write It!

As you go over the words in self-recitation, you can turn on multiple strength learning. If you learn a word with your eyes alone, you'll be using just one third of your sensory learning channels for mastering new words. The word may remain with you only briefly. Why not use all-out VAK learning-Visual, Auditory, and Kinesthetic?

College students are advised, "Use your eyes in learning then add your ears and muscles."

See it!

Say it!

Hear it!

Write it!

1. Use your eyes as you see and reread the word and its meaning. "photograph" the word with your mind. Close your eyes and see it! Then check your mental image with the card.

2. Say the word aloud or in a whisper. Now you've added kinesthetic (muscular) learning as you involve the muscles of your throat, lips, and tongue.

3. Strengthen learning with your ears as you hear yourself say it. Now you've brought to bear your auditory memory.

4. Add kinesthetic learning again as you write down the word and its meaning. You've now involved motor memory, which in many students is the strongest of the learning channels. If spelling is a problem, you might print the trouble spots in large letters or colored ink.

This is four-way reinforcement. The variety itself helps you recall. The change of pace-eyes, voice, ears, pencil-keeps you alert and increases absorption.

Keep your current working group to words manageable. An unwieldy pack of flashcards or a long, forbidding list may seem overwhelming. You might prefer to work on words in groups of five. Short term goals, readily reachable, will bring you a sense of accomplishment and satisfaction.

How to Retain Longer Through Spaced Reviews

You can remember longer simply by the timing of your reviews. You can plan your first review to minimize forgetting. Suppose you read an assignment today. When will forgetting take its greatest toll? If you are typical, the greatest loss will be within one day. Arrange your first review to check this drop. Place it from 12 to 24 hours after you study. Reinforce immediately what you learned, and you will remember it much longer.

7.30 Reading Selection
Reading Skills Related to Physical Education and Health

Purpose:

To itemize skills necessary for success in physical education/health.

Directions:

Read the following and discuss:

Skills that the successful physical education/health student should possess include the ability to:
1. Identify recognize and interpret abbreviations and symbols.
2. Define, identify and illustrate equipment.
3. Follow directions.
4. Read charts and diagrams.
5. Recall procedures and regulations.
6. Visualize performance.
7. Determine sequence of steps in team activities.

Purpose for Reading:

Determine the purpose for reading. Is it to follow directions? Is it to define new terms? Is it to interpret a chart? Is it for recall of main idea? Is it to explain directions for a game or activity?

Rate of Reading:

Adjust your rate of reading based on the objective for reading. If you are previewing a unit or chapter, you may read lightly and quickly. If you are reading charts or tables that are technical, read carefully and slowly. If you are reading to recall directions for a sport or activity read deliberately and slowly.

Vocabulary:

The vocabulary in physical education will deal with sports terms, rules, equipment and procedures. Treat all new words as in any subject and teach them as introduced earlier in this chapter. Try to illustrate or help the student visualize new terms whenever possible. Health vocabulary will be similar to the science vocabulary. Refer to that section as a reference.

Follow-up:
1. Identify the units of study in physical education and health at your school.
2. Review the vocabulary associated with the units.
3. Create flashcards, games, and vocabulary-centered activities that you can use with your tutees.

7.31 Reading Selection
Reading in Physical Education and Health Education

Purpose:

To provide information on the need for reading reinforcement in P.E.

Directions:

Read the following and discuss:

Physical education teachers can also be involved with the teaching of reading. In the event that they are charged with teaching a class in health, they may be dealing with scientific writing in textbooks and various pamphlets and current materials pertinent to current sociological and health problems.

The teacher may give the student insight into acquiring reading skills by pointing out the parallel to acquiring athletic skills.

Physical education can also be an impetus to wide reading for further information and for pleasure. Books as well as sports might be discussed in class. One coach reported:

Suppose the coach is idolized by some boy in a depressed neighborhood. He might say, "Jim come on into my office. I have this book. Can you look it over, read it, and see how you like it?" You like the kid. The kid thinks that now you talk to him! You might have given him a reading interest-a habit, maybe. You may have helped to keep him off the streets. It just might work.... I regard this as a very important part of teaching physical education and coaching. If you select books carefully, books about techniques, you're going to have more playing power in your students. Television is bringing sports events to millions, many ill-informed persons. Through books, students broaden their backgrounds, and add to their enjoyment as spectators.

There is not any subject in the curriculum that does not require the student to use reading skills in some way. There is not any subject that does not use reading profitably for enrichment. The "moral" is that reading instruction must include content. Reading cannot be taught in a vacuum, or relegated to one subject. Rather, it permeates the curriculum.

7.32 Reading Selection
Applying Tutoring Principles to the P.E. Program

Purpose:
To provide structure for P.E. tutors.

Directions:
Read the following and discuss:

The purpose of providing tutors for the physical education program is twofold:

1. Individualized and small group attention can be focused on younger participants (grades 7-9 and younger) at a time when physical development may vary as does performance.
2. Exposure to a variety of sports and activities can be increased in the program by training the tutors to supervise small groups of students that rotate between assigned sports or activity stations.

The structure of the program may vary depending on the season, the size of class, and available equipment.

Approximately two or three tutors should be assigned per P.E. class. It would be helpful to have one male and one female.

The daily routine should consist of an exercise program that lasts 7-10 minutes and participation in a sport or activity for which a skill test is designed.

Sport rotations should be planned early to enable you to be prepared for the sport or activity for which you are responsible.

	Tutor A	Tutor B	Tutor C
Week 1	Badminton Group 1	Ping Pong Group 2	Shuffleboard Group 3
Week 2	Badminton Group 3	Ping Pong Group 1	Shuffleboard Group 2
Week 3	Badminton Group 1	Ping Pong Group 2	Shuffleboard Group 3

Tutor Instruction: General Format

Monday:
1. Exercise
2. Introduce new sport
   A. Rules
   B. Important vocabulary terms
   C. Display equipment
   D. Demonstrate
   E. Student practice

Tuesday:
1. Exercise
2. Participate in sport or activity

Wednesday:
1. Exercise
2. Participate in sport or activity

Thursday:
1. Exercise
2. Set up tournament type of competition for each group.

Friday:
1. Exercise
2. Skills and/or written test
3. Complete competition

Requirements For Tutors:
1. Consistent attendance
2. Punctuality
3. Prepared for instruction
4. Dressed out

Suggested Small Area Sports

Indoors	Outdoors	Depends on Resource
Ping Pong	Softball	Bowling
Shuffleboard	Soccer	Handball
Weightlifting	Tennis	Fencing
Wrestling	Touch football	Golf
Dance	Archery	Sailing
Gymnastics	Horseshoes	Fishing
Self-defense	Lacrosse	Horseback riding
Boxing	Frisbee	Bicycling
Wiffleball	Kite flying	Swimming
Rope climbing	Kickball	Billiards
	Skateboard	Volleyball
	Tetherball	Badminton
	Baseball	Surfing
	Croquet	Rope jumping

7.33 Reading Selection

Reading Skills Related to Music

Purpose:

To itemize skills necessary for success in music.

Directions:

Read the following and discuss:

Skills that the successful music student should possess include the ability to:

1. Identify, recognize and demonstrate specialized vocabulary.
2. Identify, recognize and explain symbols.
3. Interpret mood and purpose of composer.
4. Relate the mood effect of text with mood effect of the sound.
5. Relate total music effect to individual experiences.
6. Identify, recognize, and relate identification terms to instruments and their parts.
7. Understand the function of the instrument in an orchestra.
8. Follow directions.
9. Recall words, notations, scores, stage direction, movement, mood, lyrics and tempo.

Purpose for Reading:

Determine your purpose for reading. Is it to follow directions? Is it to determine mood and tempo of a given selection? Is it to interpret symbols? Is it to define the technical vocabulary? Is it for pleasure or enrichment?

Rate of Reading:

The purpose for reading will affect the rate with which you should read. If the material or score is new, read carefully and slowly. Preview the material quickly if you are just doing a light overview, but if the purpose is for recall and demonstration, be deliberate and slow in your approach to the reading.

Vocabulary:

Music vocabulary can be very technical as in science for it involves symbols and the accurate interpretation of those symbols. It also can be like a foreign language as the vocabulary is peculiar to the subject of music alone. For these reasons, handle the vocabulary as you would in either foreign language, science or even math where many symbols are used. Refer to those sections in this chapter. Teach and reinforce the vocabulary as introduced in the beginning of this chapter.

7.34 Reading Selection
Reading in Music

Purpose:

To provide information upon to which to base tutoring instruction in music.

Directions:

Read the following and discuss:

Music, as a subject, divides into five areas as they pertain to clusters of reading skills. The first area is the student's ability to read musical notation and to interpret music symbols. Usually at the high school level little is taught in this area except to recognize various symbols and to distinguish one from the other. For instance, students are taught the difference between a whole note and a half note and such musical symbols as the clef sign, key signature, rests, and so on. However, little is done to help them read music as they would read print—for meaning. That is, students are not given instruction in being able to hear in their minds the melody from the printed representation of the music. In practice, then, the first area of music instruction resembles the symbolic aspect of mathematical vocabulary the recognition of the parts and symbols that comprise a musical score.

The second area encompasses a technical vocabulary, usually consisting of Italianate words. Knowledge of this technical vocabulary also helps students to interpret a musical score in both vocal and instrumental music. Words such as andante, allegro, forte, pianissimo comprise this type of vocabulary.

Musical theory is the third area. Usually, only a small number of students who wish to specialize in it embark on this more advanced level of music. This aspect of musical instruction is not taught in all high schools but is taught in some large city and suburban schools. Tirro points out rather picturesquely the intense nature of reading required of music theory texts:

Music theory texts are almost in a class unto themselves. Very similar to an algebra text or a geometry problem book where each letter, number, and sign must be carefully considered, tasted, chewed, swallowed and retched like a cow's cud. It becomes obvious that one does not really read a theory book; one grapples with it in a life and death struggle.

The fourth area resembles the type of reading required of English and social studies. It includes reading for background and enrichment to investigate aspects of musical history and the lives of composers. Historical content and biographical material are the key types in this area.

The fifth area involves the area of musical criticism. Current newspaper writing about musical events includes comments by music editors and critics. Obviously such material is written with a specific point of view. The reading must apply criteria of evaluating the criticism just as he would read critically in any subject. As applied to a critical analysis of either music or literature, the reader will need to check out the background qualification and point of view of the writer. The student will also check the use of words which may be used to present a specific impression as well as the writer's grasp of the subject.

7.35 Skill Practice

Lesson: Basic Reading in/on Music

Purpose:

To give practice in designing and teaching a lesson in music.

Materials Needed:

1. This short lesson material.
2. Set of cutouts notes and clef signs.
3. 24 x 36 sheet of poster tagboard as a gameboard with staff lines drawn on it for placement of notes.

Directions:

Read and study the following material. Ask for help if you need it.

Music is notated on what is called the great or grand staff. The notes are placed on different lines and spaces on the staff (see illustration). Musical sound embodies both pitch (the high-low characteristic) and rhythm (the long-short characteristic).

Pitch is denoted by placing different notes on different lines and spaces. Names are given to the lines and spaces which correspond to the different notes or pitch levels. The higher you move up the staff, the higher the pitch of the note placed thereon.

The Treble and Bass Clef

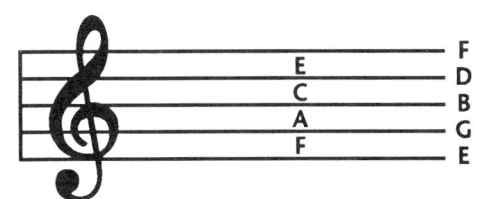

Using the treble clef. Also called the C clef.

Using the bass clef. Also called the F clef.

Two numbers placed after the clef sign near the beginning of the staff indicate the meter and rhythm. The upper number gives the number of beats per measure (meter). The lower number indicates the type of note that will receive one beat (rhythm). The rhythm and meter determine how fast or how slow a piece of music will be played or sung. See the illustration below. A line drawn vertically across the staff is used to separate the measures.

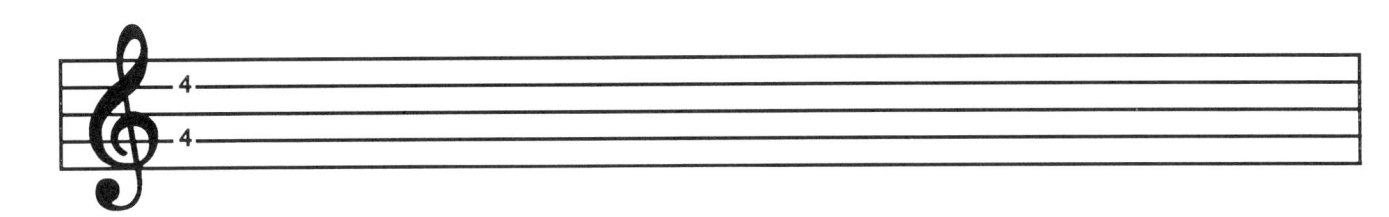

Time Signature Chart

Time Signature	4/4	8/8	2/2	16/16
Whole Note	4 beats	8 beats	2 beats	16 beats
Half Note	2 beats	4 beats	1 beat	8 beats
Quarter Note	1 beat	2 beats	1/2 beat	4 beats
Eighth Note	1/2 beat	1 beat	1/4 beat	2 beats

When you think you understand the information given in this lesson, see if you can answer these questions. This will help you understand the material you have just studied. If you don't know the answer, go back to the material and study it again. Answer your group of questions, or you may answer all the groups if you want to.

Group I

1. What is the purpose of this lesson?
2. What does the treble clef look like?
3. What does the bass clef look like?
4. Where is the time signature located?
5. Which number in the time signature gives the number of beats per measure?

Group II

1. How many beats would be in a measure of 3/4 time?
2. How many beats would be in a measure of 6/8 time?
3. Look at the example of the treble clef. Which note is pitched higher G or D?
4. Draw a staff on your paper. Now, place the following note on it.
    A. Half note on F
    B. Whole note on high E
    C. Eighth note on A
    D. Two quarter notes on C
    E. Quarter note on low B
    F. Whole note on high D

Group III

1. Use quarter notes and eighth notes for the correct number of beats in a measure of 4/4 time.
2. How could a measure of 2/4 time be written to give a feeling of 6/8 time?
3. Write four measures of any combination of notes in 6/8 time.
4. Change the four measures in number 3 to 3/4 time.

Chapter 8
Recordkeeping Functions in Tutoring

Chapter Concepts:
1. Certain records are essential to the monitoring of the tutoring program.
2. Accurate monitoring of the tutoring program will yield day-to-day progress information.

Chapter Objectives:
1. To provide information regarding the tutoring program in a structured format.
2. To train you to use the records accurately and efficiently.

Chapter Description:
This chapter deals with the purpose and use of specific record forms. An example of each form is included in the chapter.

Chapter Vocabulary:
tally, progress, drill, percentage, profile

Contents

8.01	Tally Sheet	Reading Selection	116
8.02	Drill Progress Record	Reading Selection	118
8.03	Weekly Grade Sheet	Reading Selection	119
8.04	Skill Game Day Record	Reading Selection	120
8.05	Game Winner Sheet	Reading Selection	121
8.06	Individual Tutee Skills Sheet	Reading Selection	122
8.07	Student Profile Sheet	Reading Selection	123

8.01 Reading Selection

Tally Sheet

Purpose:

To provide a record of all correct, incorrect and helped responses daily.

Directions:

1. Record the date of the session on the left side of the blocks.
2. You may wish to note the material you are using on the tally sheet, but it is not required.
3. Each block represents one response from the tutee.
4. Every time a correct answer is given, record a slanted line (/) in the block for a correct response.
5. Encourage the tutees to give answers no faster than tutors can mark them.
6. Place an (h) in the block if you had to help.
7. If the tutees are unable to answer correctly, the tutor may provide the answer and move on.
8. If the response was incorrect, leave the block open—unmarked.
9. Go back to any questions that were answered incorrectly in order to provide a second opportunity for success on that item.
10. The tutee or the tutor may do the recording as responses are given. That is the tutor's choice.
11. Tutors should calculate the grade.
12. If the tutee gets 90% to 94% of the answers correct, they need only brief reminders of clues when they have trouble.
13. The object is to complete as many problems as accurately as possible, thus achieving a feeling of satisfaction and success.
14. At the end of the session, draw a line from the left side of the page to the right side under the last set of blocks dividing work of that day from the others.
15. Give one point for every correct answer; give 1/2 point for helps.
16. Tally the number correct, helped, incorrect and place that information on the right side.
17. Convert the total correct responses out of the total number possible to a percent.
18. Place the grade on the drill progress record (8.02).
19. At the end of the week those daily percent grades are averaged and placed on the weekly grade sheet (8.03).

Note: If the right conditions are present, tutoring will appear almost rhythmical—with a deliberate fast pace. If tutors watch each problem or follow carefully while tutees read, they will learn along with tutees. Neither tutee or tutor should appear bored or restless.

There should be no waiting periods—of even one or two minutes. You should have your session materials in front of you and ready when the tutee arrives. You should proceed to drill without interruption and continue until time to stop.

Chapter 8 — Recordkeeping Functions in Tutoring

Tally Sheet

Name _____ Date: _____

    1 2 3 4 5 6 7 8 9 10 11 12 13 14 15 16 17 18 19 20   Total %

___ ☐☐☐☐☐☐☐☐☐☐☐☐☐☐☐☐☐☐☐☐ /h _____

    1 2 3 4 5 6 7 8 9 10 11 12 13 14 15 16 17 18 19 20   Total %

___ ☐☐☐☐☐☐☐☐☐☐☐☐☐☐☐☐☐☐☐☐ /h _____

    1 2 3 4 5 6 7 8 9 10 11 12 13 14 15 16 17 18 19 20   Total %

___ ☐☐☐☐☐☐☐☐☐☐☐☐☐☐☐☐☐☐☐☐ /h _____

    1 2 3 4 5 6 7 8 9 10 11 12 13 14 15 16 17 18 19 20   Total %

___ ☐☐☐☐☐☐☐☐☐☐☐☐☐☐☐☐☐☐☐☐ /h _____

    1 2 3 4 5 6 7 8 9 10 11 12 13 14 15 16 17 18 19 20   Total %

___ ☐☐☐☐☐☐☐☐☐☐☐☐☐☐☐☐☐☐☐☐ /h _____

    1 2 3 4 5 6 7 8 9 10 11 12 13 14 15 16 17 18 19 20   Total %

___ ☐☐☐☐☐☐☐☐☐☐☐☐☐☐☐☐☐☐☐☐ /h _____

    1 2 3 4 5 6 7 8 9 10 11 12 13 14 15 16 17 18 19 20   Total %

___ ☐☐☐☐☐☐☐☐☐☐☐☐☐☐☐☐☐☐☐☐ /h _____

    1 2 3 4 5 6 7 8 9 10 11 12 13 14 15 16 17 18 19 20   Total %

___ ☐☐☐☐☐☐☐☐☐☐☐☐☐☐☐☐☐☐☐☐ /h _____

/ = Correct
h = help
blank = incorrect

8.02 Reading Selection

Drill Progress Record

Purpose:

To record daily progress and provide a method of evaluation by graphing results.

Directions:

1. Record daily the date you are working, one line per day. Record on the left.
2. Record the material you used that day. Include the number of the item, code, page number, lesson number, etc.
3. Place a large dot at the correct spot on the graph that represents the percent.
4. Record the percent in numerical form to the far right of the graph.
5. Connect the dots daily. When you finish one sheet, start a new sheet, always stapling the sheets together with the most recent on top.
6. Review the progress of your tutee with your supervising teacher.

Drill Progress Record

Name: _____

Date	Materials Used	70%	75%	80%	85%	90%	95%	100%

Chapter 8 Recordkeeping Functions in Tutoring

8.03 Reading Selection
Weekly Grade Sheet

Purpose:

To provide a record of the student's weekly grade and subsequent six- or nine-week and semester grade.

Directions:

1. At the beginning of each nine weeks list all the dates for each week for that period.
2. Record the weekly grade. After adding up the total for each day from the week and getting an average.
3. At the end of the nine weeks, average the grades: divide by the number of weeks and record the grade.
4. At the end of each semester or trimester, average the nine weeks' grades to record the semester or trimester grade.
5. The tutoring grade should comprise a specific percentage of the student's content class work. Classroom teacher: 15%-20% is a reasonable consideration.
6. Record comments by each week as they are appropriate and helpful.

Weekly Grade Sheet

Quarter:_____ Semester:_____
Student:_____ Tutor:_____

Week Ending	Grade	Comments
1		
2		
3		
4		
5		
6		
7		
8		
9		
9 Week Average		
Semester Avereage		

8.04 Reading Selection
Skill Game Day Record

Purpose:

To enable you to keep a record of skill games played.

Directions:

1. Use one sheet per semester.
2. You are responsible for recording the results for the game group for that day, regardless of whether they are your tutees.
3. Record the date the game was played.
4. Record the name of the game.
5. Record the skill of the game played. Check the skill sheet if you don't know.
6. Record a name on the winner's sheet for your game (8.05).

Reminders:

1. No game should be repeated twice in a row.
2. Be sure to vary the games for your group so that each student plays a game specific to an indicated skill needed.
3. Do not play a game for which you are not prepared.
4. Directions for the games should be kept in folders that can be checked out for your convenience.
5. Select games that you enjoy and that you think the tutees will enjoy. If you are enthused so will the students be.
6. Be careful with game parts and replace material in appropriate location.

Skill Game Day Record

Name: _____   Tutor: _____

Date	Game	Skill	Winner

Elizabeth Sabrinsky Foster, Ed.D.

Chapter 8 | Recordkeeping Functions in Tutoring

8.05 Reading Selection
Game Winner Sheet

Purpose:

To provide a record of each winner for the skill game played.

Directions:

1. Record the winner's name, the date, the name of game, and the tutor's name.

2. Clip the slip to the next Monday's Tally Sheet in the tutee folder.

3. Add 5 points to the weekly total before averaging.

Game Winner

Name: _____   is awarded 5 points to tutoring

Date: _____   for playing _____

Leader _____

Game Winner

Name: _____   is awarded 5 points to tutoring

Date: _____   for playing _____

Leader _____

Game Winner

Name: _____   is awarded 5 points to tutoring

Date: _____   for playing _____

Leader _____

Individual Tutee Skills Sheet

8.06 Reading Selection

Purpose:
To provide a list of skills on which you should work with the tutees. To organize the skills and record tutoring sessions involved with the skills.

Directions:
1. Look at the student's need sheet, or teacher list, and record all skills needed.
2. For every game played, based on an identified skill, write the date of the game.
3. Every time there is a tutoring session, place a checkmark on the session column.
4. At the end of the year, total the number of sessions tutored per skill.

Individual Tutee Skills Sheet

Tutee: _____

Tutor: _____

Date: _____

Content Subject: _____

Information taken from: _____

Textbook inventory: ____yes ____ no

Skill Indicated List in Order	Skill Games	Tutoring Sessions	Approximate Total Sessions

8.07 Reading Selection
Student Profile Sheet

Purpose:
To provide an overview of the student receiving tutoring services. To provide a get acquainted activity for you and your tutee.

Directions:
1. Read a completed interest survey completed by the tutee.
2. Summarize likes/dislikes/family information/hobbies, and so forth by writing them in the appropriate place on the profile sheet.
3. Use this information to "get to know" your students.

Student Name _____

Tutor _____

Age _____

Grade _____

Subject _____

Courses liked: _____

Courses disliked: _____

Things student *really* likes to do: _____
_____

Things student dislikes doing: _____
_____

Family: _____

What social activities?: _____

Goals: _____

Comments: _____
_____
_____

Chapter 9
Evaluation In Tutoring

Chapter Concepts:

1. Evaluation is a necessary element of any program to assess the progress of the program and participants.
2. It is important to assess the progress of all program components.

Chapter Objectives:

1. To provide information on various types of evaluation tools.
2. To prepare you to complete evaluation forms.
3. To provide information on how evaluation data can be used.

Chapter Description:

This chapter describes the various evaluation tools used to demonstrate development and progress of the program and program participants.

Chapter Vocabulary:

responsibility, developmental, placement, achievement, standardized, diagnostic, evaluation, critique

Contents

9.01	Definitions of Evaluation Tools	Reading Assignment	126
9.02	Pre-Post Evaluation of Self	Evaluation F-1	127
9.03	Tutor Evaluation of Tutees	Evaluation F-2	128
9.04	Evaluation of Tutors	Evaluation F-3	129
9.05	Teacher Evaluation of Tutor	Evaluation F-4	130
9.06	Teacher Evaluation for P.E. Tutors	Evaluation F-5	131

9.01 Reading Assignment

Definitions of Evaluation Tools

Purpose:

To provide testing definitions, use of information and examples of evaluation on forms in tutoring.

Directions:

Read the following information and discuss.

1. **Standardized Test:** This type of test is one that is measured by comparing the testing group to a norm group, usually a national norm. Test scores are compared and evaluated on those norms. Tests such as the C.A.T. (California Achievement Test) or C.T.B.S. (Comprehensive Test of Basic Skills) are standardized "achievement" tests. Standardized tests are developed for achievement, diagnostics, reading, aptitude and other types of data.

2. **Diagnostic Test:** This type of test is used to determine what strengths or weaknesses a person might have in a certain skill area or subject.

3. **Achievement Test:** This type of test is one developed to determine how much the student has achieved in a certain skill or subject, as compared to a national norm.

4. **Reading Test:** This type of test is developed to provide information on the reading ability and level of the student. It is a valuable aid in diagnosis.

5. **Placement Test:** This type of test is usually produced and published by a commercial company for the purpose of placing the student into a level of a program. The appropriate level of entry into the program is indicated by analyzing the test results. The level numbers for placement usually have nothing to do with the reading level or grade level. The numbers merely provide a means of having several books dealing with the same skill, but on different developmental levels.

Test Responsibility:

The responsibility of determining appropriate tests, diagnosis of those tests and placement into programs is that of the classroom instructor. Any questions you may have about testing information should be directed to the instructor with whom you are working.

Testing of the Tutors:

There could be several evaluation instruments administered in the fall as pre-tests and in the spring as post-tests. They have nothing to do with grades. The purpose of the pre-post test program is to provide statistical data indicating the development of the tutor in areas of communication skills, academic skills and tutoring skills. The results of these tools will always be available to you. Please ask if you have questions.

Evaluation Forms Used in Tutoring:

Form 1 Pre-Post Evaluation of Self
(Tutor Completion)

Form 2 Tutor Evaluation of Tutees
(Tutor Completion)

Form 3 Evaluation of Tutors
(Tutee Completion)

Form 4 Teacher Evaluation of Tutor
(Teacher Completion)

Form 5 Evaluation for P.E. Tutors
(Teacher Completion)

Chapter 9 — Evaluation in Tutoring

9.02 Evaluation F-I

Pre-Post Evaluation of Self
(Tutor Completion)

Purpose:
To allow you to review your work and effort individually as well as to give feedback to the supervising instructor.

Directions:
Place the number on the appropriate blank that best describes how you see yourself in relation to the items listed. Scoring: 1 = weak, 2 = need help, 3 = average, 4 = strong, and 5 = excellent.

Pre-   Post-
_____ _____ 1. Listening ability.
_____ _____ 2. Positive attitude.
_____ _____ 3. Willingness to help.
_____ _____ 4. Able to control behavior of tutee.
_____ _____ 5. Able to motivate tutee.
_____ _____ 6. Enthusiasm-consistent.
_____ _____ 7. Understanding your duties as a tutee.
_____ _____ 8. Your confidence in your ability to tutor.
_____ _____ 9. Patience.
_____ _____ 10. Your commitment to helping.
_____ _____ 11. Recordkeeping ability.
_____ _____ 12. Efficiency.
_____ _____ 13. Use of time.
_____ _____ 14. Completing "outside" assignments.
_____ _____ 15. Attendance.
_____ _____ 16. Learning new things (techniques, skills).
_____ _____ 17. Organizing the game on game day.
_____ _____ 18. Managing the group for game day.
_____ _____ 19. Cooperation with the supervising teacher.
_____ _____ 20. Your ability to get the "correct" response from the tutee.
_____ _____ Total 1-10 (Affective)
_____ _____ Total 11-20 Cognitive)
_____ _____ Combination Total

_____
Total Total

9.03 Evaluation F-2

Tutor Evaluation of Tutees
(Tutor Completion)

Purpose:

To allow you to review your work with the tutee as well as provide feedback.

Directions:

During your experiences as a tutor, you and your partners worked closely on learning many new skills. You probably can remember a lot about what happened during your tutoring sessions. Below are statements that may describe your working relationship with or your perceptions of your tutoring partner. For each of the statements, circle the letter A = Always True, F = Frequently True, O = Often True, S = Seldom True, and N = Never True) that most nearly reflects the truth of that statement for you, as you remember your partner during the tutoring sessions. Remember that this relating scale is intended to describe only the times that you and the tutee were tutoring together. Complete one form per tutee.

Cognitive

A F O S N 1. I had the feeling that the student knew what was to be done.

A F O S N 2. The student took responsibility for learning the materials in a lesson.

A F O S N 3. It seemed to me that the student took the work seriously.

A F O S N 4. The student gave answers clearly and carefully.

A F O S N 5. I would like to work with my partner again.

A F O S N 6. I thought my student did a good job.

A F O S N 7. The student seemed to be in control at all times.

A F O S N 8. The student had a positive attitude toward learning during our sessions.

A F O S N 9. The student did everything possible to help us finish on time.

A F O S N 10. The student responded to reinforcement and motivation techniques.

Affective

A F O S N 1. The student was a likable person.

A F O S N 2. I had the feeling that here was a person who I could really trust.

A F O S N 3. It was easy to talk to the student.

A F O S N 4. I always had the feeling that I was only another student as far as my partner was concerned

A F O S N 5. The student expressed feelings openly with me.

A F O S N 6. The student treated me with respect.

A F O S N 7. The student did not make fun of me.

A F O S N 8. The student made comments to me that made me feel good.

A F O S N 9. The student listened carefully to what I had to say.

Chapter 9 — Evaluation in Tutoring

9.04 Evaluation F-3

Evaluation of Tutors
(Tutee Completion)

Purpose:
To provide feedback from the tutees on their perceptions of the tutor.

Directions:
Please place one of the following numbers (1 = always, 2 = most of the time, 3 = never, 4 = don't know) on the line in front of each statement for **each academic quarter**.

Tutor: _____

Tutee's Initials: _____

Date: _____

Supervising Teacher: _____

Quarter

1   2   3   4

___ ___ ___ ___ 1. My tutor is prepared with materials for tutoring.

___ ___ ___ ___ 2. My tutor enjoys tutoring.

___ ___ ___ ___ 3. My tutor is interested in me.

___ ___ ___ ___ 4. My tutor is well organized.

___ ___ ___ ___ 5. My tutor explains "why" we do what we do in tutoring.

___ ___ ___ ___ 6. My tutor lets me know my daily and weekly grades.

___ ___ ___ ___ 7. My tutor knows and understands the material used in tutoring.

___ ___ ___ ___ 8. My tutor is helpful to me in learning.

___ ___ ___ ___ 9. My tutor is patient.

___ ___ ___ ___ 10. My tutor explains "how" to do assignments in tutoring.

___ ___ ___ ___ 11. My tutor lets me ask questions whenever I feel I need to do so.

___ ___ ___ ___ 12. My tutor explains things so that I can understand.

___ ___ ___ ___ 13. My tutor gives me challenging work.

___ ___ ___ ___ 14. My tutor encourages me.

___ ___ ___ ___ 15. My tutor listens to me.

9.05 Evaluation F-4

Teacher Evaluation of Tutor
(Teacher Completion)

Purpose:
To provide feedback from your supervising teacher to you regarding your performance.

Directions:
Please assess a point value for each of the following items:

Grade	A	A-	B+	B	C	D	F	N/O
Percentage	95	92	90	85	80	75	60	
Points	5.0	4.6	4.5	4.2	4.0	3.8	3.0	

Date: _____   Tutor: _____

Hour: _____   Subject: _____

_____ 1. The tutor is prepared.

_____ 2. The tutor has necessary materials available.

_____ 3. The tutor demonstrates acceptable knowledge of basic tutoring concepts.

_____ 4. The tutor presents material in an appropriate sequence.

_____ 5. The tutor gives clear directions.

_____ 6. The tutor uses positive reinforcement.

_____ 7. The tutor manages the tutee's behavior.

_____ 8. The tutor uses immediate feedback.

_____ 9. The tutor maintains eye to eye contact.

_____ 10. The tutor uses affective responses.

_____ 11. The tutor keeps the tutee on task.

_____ 12. The tutor actively involves the tutee.

_____ 13. The tutor uses the timer consistently.

_____ 14. The tutee appears interested during the session.

_____ 15. The tutor appears interested during the session.

_____ 16. The tutor uses non-tutoring time constructively.

_____ 17. The tutor utilizes entire session.

_____ 18. The tutor keeps records up-to-date.

_____ 19. The tutor cooperates with the teacher.

_____ 20. The tutor has consistent attendance.   Absent_____

_____ Total points per 9 weeks.   Grade _____

Comments:

Chapter 9   Evaluation in Tutoring

9.06 Evaluation F-5

Evaluation for P.E. Tutors

Directions:

Please assess a point value for each of the following items. Scale: 5 points per item; 100 points possible. N/O = not observed.

Grade	A	A-	B+	B	C	D	F	N/O
Centile	95	92	90	85	80	75	60	
Points	5.0	4.6	4.5	4.2	4.0	3.8	3.0	

Date: _____ Tutor: _____

Hour _____ Subject: _____

_____ 1. The tutor is prepared for the assignment.

_____ 2. The tutor has equipment and materials ready.

_____ 3. The tutor appears organized.

_____ 4. The tutor demonstrates acceptable knowledge of basic tutoring concepts.

_____ 5. The tutor demonstrates acceptable knowledge of sports during instruction.

_____ 6. The tutor provides a consistent exercise program.

_____ 7. The tutor actively involves *all* members of the group.

_____ 8. The tutor keeps members of group on task.

_____ 9. The tutor gives clear directions.

_____ 10. The tutor dresses out.

_____ 11. The tutor uses positive reinforcement.

_____ 12. The tutor manages the behavior of the group.

_____ 13. The tutor manages personal behavior effectively.

_____ 14. The tutor uses immediate feedback.

_____ 15. The tutor uses affective responses.

_____ 16. The tutor appears interested during *all* sessions.

_____ 17. The tutor utilizes entire P.E. time block constructively.

_____ 18. The tutor cooperates with instructor.

_____ 19. The tutor replaces equipment and materials after use.

_____ 20. The tutor has consistent attendance.   Absent _____

_____ Total points per 9-weeks.   Grade _____

Comments:

Appendix
Test Answers

1.03 Tutoring Pre-Test

1. A	6. A	11. A	16. A
2. B	7. A	12. A	17. A
3. A	8. A	13. A	18. A
4. B	9. A	14. B	19. A
5. A	10. A	15. B	20. A

1.06 Success/Failure Questionnaire

1. Abraham Lincoln
2. Richard Bach, author of Jonathan Livingston Seagull
3. John F. Kennedy
4. Winston Churchill
5. Flip Wilson
6. Madame Curie, the woman scientist who isolated radium
7. Ludwig van Beethoven
8. Bobby Kennedy
9. Lucille Ball
10. "All in the Family"
11. Edward Gibson, one of the 3 astronauts in the Sky Lab III mission—he was the science pilot.
12. Joe Namath-during this game, he also threw 3 touchdown passes and led the New York Jets to a victory over the Oakland Raiders 27-23. That day the Jets won their first AFL championship.
13. Henry Aaron
14. Napoleon
15. Milton S. Hershey, Hershey Chocolate Company
16. President Gerald R. Ford
17. Dr. Story Hargrave, one of 11 scientist astronauts
18. Johnny Unitas, one of the great quarterbacks of all time
19. Walt Disney
20. Babe Ruth, perhaps the most famous baseball player who ever lived
21. President Jimmy Carter

2.04 Lincoln Logs Can Help-Roles

1. **The Know it All**—"I'm the expert. I know what a house is supposed to look like. I'm going to make sure you-re going to build a good house. I'll show you how to make a good house."

2. **The Care Less Bore**—"I couldn't care less what you do. I won't be rude to you so I'll give you a little help. But don't bother me too much.

3. **The Great Pretender**—"I really don't know much about building houses. But I'll pretend I do. I don't want you to know I've never built a house. I make a lot of mistakes at your expense."

4. **The Excited Novice**—"Wow! This is terrific! Aren't you glad we got this chance! Everything you do is great! I'm new at this but you're terrific. I'm terrific. This is terrific."

5. **The Pessimist**—No matter what we do, it won't be right. You can try to build a house. Non one will like it. If I can help you, I know you won't like me. If we do it together, we'll end up fighting. But go ahead anyway. Try if you want to."

6. **The Critic**—"I've built a few houses. Nothing you do is right. I'm very critical of your ability and want it to look the way mine always have."

7. **The Caring Helper**—"I want to help you solve your own problem. If there is anything I can do to help you build your house, I'd like to. I'm confident in your ability to build a house that meets with your satisfaction."

3.01 Communication Pre-Test

1. F	7. T	13. F
2. T	8. F	14. T
3. T	9. T	15. T
4. T	10. F	16. T
5. T	11. T	17. T
6. T	12. T	18. F

Chapter 9 — Evaluation in Tutoring

3.04 What is Listening?

1. **False.** Listening and hearing are not the same. Hearing is having the sound waves enter your ears. Listening is using the brain to focus on those sounds and put them to work.
2. **False.** 70 percent of your waking time is spent taking in information.
3. **False.** 45 percent of our time we are listening.
4. **False.** People of all levels of intelligence have to be taught good listening skills.
5. **False.** Listening and reading use some of the same skills, but listening requires other, different skills.
6. **True.** The average speaker uses 150 to 175 words per minute. But your brain can hear at that rate and still have much time left over.

3.05 What is Listening?

1. False: Listening and hearing are not the same. Hearing is having the sound waves enter your ears. Listening is using the brain to focus on those sounds and putting them to work.
2. False: 70 percent of your waking time is spent taking in information.
3. False: 45 percent of our time we are listening.
4. False: People of all levels of intelligence have to be taught good listening skills. Without these skills any person's ability to understand and retain knowledge will be low.
5. False: Listening and reading use some of the same skills. But listening requires other, different skills. That's what this book will show you.
6. True: The average speaker uses 150-175 words per minute. But your brain can hear at that rate and still have much time left over. This difference between talking and thinking has results that you will hear about later.

3.08 Suggested Rumors

(A) In the year 2042 the Purple Martians from Yukatana came to earth. They were so ugly with purple faces, 9 arms, 3 heads, 6 ears, bananas for legs and raisins for toes. After landing in San Francisco on the freeway, there was an instant mass of crashes- twelve dozen autos and trucks collided into the green and black 12-pronged space ship. The Purple Martians were called Polowanos and spoke like they were in echo chambers. There first words were, "What's up, Doc?"

(B) Matilda Tinklehorn, who was 93 years old, lived in Tunesville, Tennessee with Tippy, her turtle. She also lived with all of her chickens, elephants and kola bears. She enjoyed surfing except her bathtub was too small and the water kept draining out the plug.

3.12 Do You Know What Your Voice Reveals?

1.T	3.T	5.7	7.T	9. T
2.T	4.T	6.T	8.T	10.T

3.17 Identify the Feeling-Suggested Answers
1. Happiness, pride
2. Sadness, loneliness
3. Embarrassment, ridicule, inept
4. Discouraged, unattractive, lonely
5. Pride, accomplished
6. Excitement, pleasure
7. Unprepared, angry
8. Unjustified
9. Embarrassed, sad, alone
10. Hopeless, distressed
11. Excited, pride
12. Hopeful, anxious
13. Defiant, determined, independent
14. Silly, easy, waste of time
15. Frustrated, overworked, exhausted involved

3.14 Practicing Roadblocks
1. Kidding, teasing
2. Diverting by passing
3. Diagnosing
4. Supporting, sympathizing
5. Praising
6. Evaluating, criticizing
7. Moralizing, preaching
8. Warning, threatening
9. Directing, ordering
10. Persuading, arguing
11. Kidding, teasing
12. Diagnosing

3.20 Using the Feeling Side-Appropriate Responses
Principle 1 Answer: C
Principle 2 Answer: A
Principle 3 Answer: C
Principle 4 Answer: A

3.21 Select the Effective Feeling Response
The following were the responses most frequently selected by a group of 200 counselors in training:
Situation 1: 1B, 2B, 3C, 4C, 5C
Situation 2: 1D, 2B, 3C, 4B, 5A

4.04 Pre-Test for Positive Reinforcement
1. C 4. C 7. C
2. C 5. D 8. D
3. C 6. C

6.11 How to begin a Lesson—Test Yourself
1. B 4. C
2. A 5. C
3. B

7.14 Worksheet for Sight Word Recognition
1. repercussion 6. jealous 11. transvection
2. solander 7. medley 12. unicorn
3. supplemental 8. mileage 13. tromper
4. ulcerous 9. navy 14. verse
5. independent 10. prevention 15. enumeration

7.15 Worksheet in Context Clue Usage
1. hysteric 4. gyroscope 7. loneliness
2. treacherous 5. accumulated 8. wisdom
3. mob 6. suppress

7.16 Worksheet for Literal Comprehension
1. Who 5. When 8. Where
2. Where 6. How 9. What
3. How 7. What 10. Where
4. What

7.17 Worksheet for Sequence Ability
1. D 5. A 9. I
2. G 6. K 10. F
3. J 7. C 11. H
4. B 8. E 12. L

About the Author

Elizabeth Sabrinsky Foster, Ed.D. has been a pioneer in peer helping for years. She has developed model peer programs which have been recognized with both state and national awards. Her own state of North Carolinia's peer helping association honored her by naming their Peer Helping Service Award after her.

The author of *Energizers and Icebreakers for All Ages and Stages,* Elizabeth also has written for numerous publications, served as editor of the *Peer Facilitator Quarterly,* co-authored an adult mentor training program, served as President of the North Carolina Peer Helpers Association, and most recently, as President of the National Peer Helpers Association.

As an educator, Elizabeth has worked extensively in areas of individualized instruction, high risk youth, reading instruction, remedial services, program design, curriculum development, and peer concepts. She has served as a classroom teacher, learning lab coordinator, reading resource coordinator, adult interaction leader, coordinator of peer programs, supervisor of curriculum, and university coordinator of middle grades education.

Certified in reading, English, counseling, mentoring, and supervision with graduate work in administration, Dr. Foster continues to view education as a life-long practice. She has extensive experience in training and consulting. She has presented dynamic programs throughout the United States, training thousands of students and adults in the development of peer programs at the elementary, middle, secondary, and adult levels.

Dr. Foster holds a B.S.Ed. degree in English from Ohio University, an M.A.Ed. in guidance and personnel services from North Carolina State University, and a doctorate in counseling from North Carolina State University. She currently holds the position as Coordinator of Middle Grades Education at East Carolina University in Greenville, North Carolina.

A Note to Students

As you complete this portion of your training, I hope you will look forward to your work as a tutor with enthusiasm and determination. You have a power within you that is uniquely yours—it is yours to share through this program. Remember to accept the frailties and strengths of your tutees as you trust that they will accept yours.

When you have questions, worries, or wonders, ask your program coordinator/trainer during your on-going training sessions. These are excellent times to reflect upon your experiences, to review the positive impact you are making, and to assess areas in which you would like to grow. You will discover many things you still do not know, but remember, it is okay not to know. Just say, "I'll find out."

Work with your fellow students to reinforce their efforts as tutors. This will help you to form your own support group which will be most helpful as you analyze your work and celebrate your successes.

If you would like to share your thoughts or reactions with me, I'd love to hear how you are doing. Please write and tell me about your program, the role you have, and the effects of your experiences. Send pictures! I love to share them with other peer helpers!

Write to me at the following:

> Dr. Elizabeth S. Foster
> School of Education
> East Carolina University
> Greenville, NC 27858

Have a wonderful experience. Know that I celebrate all of your hard work and dedication with you. Your contributions will be your reward!

A Note to Leaders

While a great deal of work has been done in the field of peer helping, it is by no means a finished task. There is still much study and work to be done. Please help in this effort by letting me know how this book is helpful, what might make it more helpful, and other resource needs you might have in training and program development.

Consulting and training services are available upon request. Information can be obtained by writing or calling:

>Dr. Elizabeth S. Foster
>School of Education
>East Carolina University
>Greenville, NC 27858
>(919) 757-6833

Our strength is developed together through networking and sharing information. Please send copies of any program results you may have from using this material as you complete each year. Don't forget to join your professional association: National Peer Helpers Association, P.O. Box 3783 Glendale, CA 91221-0783.

Acknowledgments

The following pages were taken from or adapted from the sources listed. It is with great appreciation that I cite these particular references.

Page 4

Adapted from "Tutoring Tips Pre-Assessment," Tutoring in Reading and Mathematics, Cluster IX Modules 19, Dade County Public Schools, Miami, Florida.

Page 6

From "The Feelings of a Student" on pp. 11-12 from "The Tutor-Student Relationship," Thomas Jr. Edward in Sidney J. Rauch (Ed.), Handbook for the Volunteer Tutor, IRA, 1969. Reprinted with permission of the author and the International Reading Association.

Page 8

From The Velveteen Rabbitt by Margery Williams, Avon Books, New York, New York.

Page 9

From Phi Delta Kappa, "The Animal School" by Dr. George H. Reavis, Asst. Superintendent, Cincinnati Public Schools, 1939-1948.

Pages 14-15

From Motivation and Personality by Abraham H. Maslow, Harper and Row, 1970.

Page 20

From Discipline in Schools, A Source Book published by North Carolina Department of Public Instruction, p. 41. Poem written by Steward Rogers.

Pages 30-32

Reprint by special permission of Tuning in Learning to Listen, published by Xerox Education Publications, 1972, Xerox Corp. (Excludes illustrations.)

Page 35

From Teaching Human Beings *101* Subversive Activities for the Classroom, pp. 143-145, by Jeffrey Schrank, Beacon Press, Boston, Massachusetts, 1972.

Page 36

From Family Weekly Magazine, "Do You Know What Your Voice Reveals?," by John E. Gibson, Feb. 21, 1971, New York, New York.

Page 37

From Becoming: A Course in Human Relating by Chester Cromwell, William Ohs, Albert Roark, and Gene Stanford, published by J. B. Lippincott Co., Philadelphia, Pennsylvania, 1975.

Page 38

From Peer Counseling: An In-Depth Look at Training Peer Helpers, pp. 99-100, by H. Dean Gray and Judith A. Tindall, Accelerated Development, Inc., Muncie, Indiana, 1978.

Page 39

From Peer Power, p. 48, by H. Dean Gray and Judith A. Tindall, Accelerated Development, Inc., Muncie, Indiana, 1978.

Chapter 9 — Evaluation in Tutoring

Pages 40-42
From Building One to One Relationships, Cluster IX Module 3, pp. 50-55, Dade County Public Schools, Miami, Florida.

Pages 42-43
Adapted from "Usefulness of Response," American Personnel and Guidance Association, Falls Church, Virginia.

Page 50
From Helping Students Develop Appropriate Behavior, Cluster IX Module 7, Dade County Public Schools.

Page 56
From Hope For The Flowers, p. 21, by Trina Paulus, Paulist Press, New York, New York, 1972.

Pages 58-60
Adapted from Teach More Faster, pp. 75-76, by Madeline Hunter, TIP Publications, El Segundo, California, 1975.

Pages 60-61
From Improved Instruction, pp. 58-67, by Madeline Hunter, TIP Publications, El Segundo, California, 1975.

Page 80
From The Handbook for the Volunteer Tutor. "Teaching Word Recognition Skills," by Harry Singer, compiled and edited by Sidney Rauch, reprinted with permission of the International Reading Association, 1969.

Page 84
From Improving Reading in Every Class, A Sourcebook for Teachers, p. 95, by Ellen Thomas and Alan Robinson, Allyn & Bacon, Inc., 1977.

Pages 57, 88
From Collected Works of Dr. James Mahaffey, Ayner, South Carolina.

Pages 85-86
From Reading Strategies for Middle and Secondary School Teachers, pp. 365-387, by Lou Burmeister, Addison Wesley Publishing Co., Menlo Park, California, 2nd ed., 1978.

Pages 94-95, 99-100, 103-104, 109, 112
From Comprehensive High School Reading Methods, by David Shepherd, Charles Merrill Publishing Co., 1973.

Pages 97-98
From The Newspaper in the Curriculum, pp. 48-49, by John Guenther, permission granted by The University of Kansas, Department of Curriculum and Instruction.

Pages 105-108
From Improving Reading in Every Class, A Sourcebook for Teachers, pp. 505-513, by Ellen Lamar Thomas and H. Alan Robinson, Allyn & Bacon, Inc., Boston, Massachusetts, 1977.

Pages 113-114
From Reading Strategies and Enrichment Activities for Grades 4-9, pp. 127-130, by Virgie McIntyre, Merrill Publishing Co., Columbus, Ohio, 1977.

Selected References

Achenback, T.M. (1974). The effects of four kinds of tutoring experience on associate responding. *American Educational Research Journal,* Volume 11, Number 4, pp. 395-405.

Allen, V.L., & Feldman, R.S. (1974). Learning through tutoring: Low-achieving children as tutors. *Journal of Experimental Education, 42,* 1-5.

Allen, V.L., & Feldman, R.S. (1976). Studies on the role of tutoring. In Allen, V.L. (ed.), *Children as teachers: Theory and research on tutoring,* pp. 113-129. New York: Academic Press.

Allen, V.L., et al. (1976). Research on children tutoring children: A critical review. *Review of Educational Research, 46*(3), 355-385.

Benard, B. (1991). The case for peers. *Peer Facilitator Quarterly, 8*(4), 20-27.

Berliner, D., & Casanova, V. (1988). Peer tutoring: A new look at a popular practice. *Instructor, 97*(5), 14-15.

Bowman, R.P. (1982). A student facilitator program: Fifth graders helping primary grade problem behavior students. Unpublished doctoral dissertation, University of Florida, Gainesville.

Bowman, R.P. (1986). Peer facilitator programs for middle graders: Students helping each other grow up. *School Counselor, 33*(3), 221-229.

Bowman, R.P., & Myrick, R.D. (1987). Effects of an elementary school peer facilitator program on children with behavior problems. *School Counselor, 34*(5), 369-378.

Brandwein, A.C., & DiVittis, A. (1985). The evaluation of a peer tutoring program: A quantitive approach. *Educational and Psychological Measurement, 45*(1), 15-27.

Britz, M.W., et al. (1989). The effects of peer tutoring on mathematics performance: A recent review. *B.C. Journal of Special Education, 13*(1), 17-33.

Brown, W. (1986). Handicapped students as peer tutors. *Academic Therapy, 22*(1), 75-79.

Brown, W.F. (1965). Student-to-student counseling for academic adjustment. *Personnel and Guidance Journal, 43,* 811-817.

Burmeister, L. (1978). *Reading strategies for middle and secondary school teachers.* Phillipines: Addison-Wesley Publishing Company, Inc.

Canfield, J., & Wells, H. (1978). *100 ways to enhance self-concept in the classroom.* Englewood Cliffs, NJ: Prentice-Hall, Inc.

Carkhuff, R.R. (1973). *The art of problem-solving*. Amherst, MA: Human Resource Development Press, Inc.

Carr, R.A., et al. (1989). Pearls among peers: A conversation with peer leaders. *Canadian Journal of Counselling, 23*(1), 5-28.

Casteel, D. (1978). *Learning to think and choose*. Santa Monica, CA: Goodyear Publishing Company, Inc.

Chrisco, I.M. (1989). Peer assistance works. *Educational Leadership, 46*(8), 31-32.

Cohen, J. (1986). Theoretical considerations of peer tutoring. *Psychology in the Schools, 23*(2), 175-186.

Colden, B., Peters, A., & Walker, G. (1976). *High intensity tutoring*. RMC Research Coooperation for Offices of Education, U.S. Department of HEW.

deRosenroll, D. (1989). A practitioner's guide to peer counselling research issues and dilemmas. *Canadian Journal of Counselling, 23*(1), 75-91.

deRosenroll, D.A., & Dey, C. (1990). A centralized approach to training peer counselors: 3 years of progress. *School Counselor, 37*(4), 304-312.

Dupont, H., Gardner, S., & and Brody, D. (1974). *Toward affective development: TAD*. Circle Pines, MN: American Guidance Service.

Earle, R.A. (1977). *Teaching reading and mathematics*. Newark, DE: International Reading Association.

Ehly, S. (1987). The present and future of peer tutoring: Some implications for special educators. *Techniques, 3*(3), 205-213.

Ehly, S.W., & Larsen, S.C. (1980). *Peer tutoring for individualized instruction*. Boston, MA: Allyn & Bacon, Inc.

Fantuzzo, J.W., et al. (1989). Effects of reciprocal peer tutoring on academic achievement and psychological adjustment: A component analysis. *Journal of Educational Psychology, 81*(2), 173-177.

Fantuzzo, J.W., et al. (1990). An evaluation of reciprocal peer tutoring across elementary school settings. *Journal of School Psychology, 28*(4), 309-323.

Fitz-Gibbon, C.T. (1988). Peer tutoring as a teaching strategy. *Educational Management and Administration, 16*(3), 217-229.

Foster, E.S. (1989). *Energizers and icebreakers: For all ages and stages*. Minneapolis, MN: Educational Media Corporation.

Foster, E.S. (1991). A case for emotional development through elementary peer helping programs. *Peer Facilitator Quarterly, 8*(4), 17-20.

Frisz, R.H. (1986). Peer counseling: Establishing a network in training and supervision. *Journal of Counseling and Development, 64*(7), 457-459.

Gartner, A., Kohler, M.C., & Riessman, F. (1971). *Children teach children: Learning by teaching*. New York: Harper and Row.

Goodlad, S., & Hirst, B. (1989). *Peer tutoring: A guide to learning by teaching*. New York: Nichols Publishing.

Gordon, T. (1970). *Parent effectiveness training: The tested new way to raise responsible children*. New York: Peter H. Wyden.

Grady, J.B. (1980). Peer counseling in the middle school: A model program. *Phi Delta Kappan, 61*(10), 710.

Greenwood, C., et al. (1989). The use of peer tutoring strategies in classroom management and educational instruction. *School Psychology Review, 17*(2), 258-275.

Gumaer, J. (1976). Training peer facilitators. *Elementary School Guidance and Counseling, 11*(1), 26-36.

Harris, J. (1987). Using three students to enhance learning in peer tutoring groups. *Techniques, 3*(2), 125-127.

Hazouri, S.P. & Smith, M.F. (1991). *Peer listening in the middle school: Training activities for students*. Minneapolis, MN: Educational Media Corporation.

Heyman, R., & Kehayan, A. (1990). Facing the issue: Students should receive course credit for peer work. *Peer Facilitator Quarterly, 8*(2), 12-14.

Hirst, B., & Goodlad, S. (1989). *Peer tutoring: A guide to learning by teaching*. East Brunswick, NJ: Nichols Publishing Co.

Hunter, M. (1975). *Teach more faster*. El Segundo, CA: Tip Publications.

Hunter, M. (1978). *Improved instruction*. El Segundo, CA: Tip Publications.

Jenkins, J., & Jenkins, L. (1985). Peer tutoring in elementary and secondary programs. *Focus on Exceptional Children, 17*(6), 1-12.

Jenkins, J.R., & Lenkins, L.M. (1987). Making peer tutoring work. *Educational Leadership, 44*(6), 64-68.

Kehayan, V.A. (1988). *Partners for change*. Ridgewood, NJ: EduPsych Outreach Center, Inc.

LaFramboise, T.D., & Big Foot, D.S. (1988). Cultural and cognitive considerations in the prevention of American Indian adolescent suicide. *Journal of Adolescence, 11*(2), 139-153.

Larsen, S.C., & Ehly, S. (1976). Peer tutoring: An aid to individual instruction. *Clearing House, 49*(6), 273-277.

Locke, D.C., & Zimmerman, N.A. (1987). Effects of peer-counseling training on psychological maturity of black students. *Journal of College Student Personnel, 28*(6), 525-532.

Lundsteen, S.W. (1979). *Listening*. Urbana, IL: ERIC Clearninghouse on Reading and Communication Skills, and the national Council of Teachers of English.

McIntyre, V. (1977). *Reading strategies and enrichment activities for grades 4-9*. Columbus, OH: Charles E. Merrill Publishing Company.

Mosher, R.L., & Sprinthall, M. (1971). Psychological education: A means to promote personal development during adolescence. *Counseling Psychologist, 2*, 3.

Myrick, R.D. (1987). *Developmental guidance and counseling: A practical approach*. Minneapolis, MN: Educational Media Corporation.

Myrick, R.D., & Bowman, R.P. (1981). *Becoming a friendly helper: A handbook for student facilitators*. Minneapolis, MN: Educational Media Corporation.

Myrick, R.D., & Bowman, R.P. (1981). *Children helping children: Teaching students to become friendly helpers*. Minneapolis, MN: Educational Media Corporation.

Myrick, R.D., & Erney, T. (1978, 1985). *Caring and sharing: Becoming a peer facilitator*. Minneapolis, MN: Educational Media Corporation.

Myrick, R.D., & Erney, T. (1979). *Youth helping youth: A handbook for training peer facilitators*. Minneapolis, MN: Educational Media Corporation.

Myrick, R.D., & Folk, B.E. (1991). *Peervention: Training peer facilitators for prevention education*. Minneapolis, MN: Educational Media Corporation.

Myrick, R.D., & Folk, B.E. (1991). *The power of peervention: A manual for the trainers of peer facilitators*. Minneapolis, MN: Educational Media Corporation.

Myrick, R.D., & Sorenson, D.L. (1988). *Peer helping: A practical guide*. Minneapolis, MN: Educational Media Corporation.

Myrick, R.D. & Sorenson, D.L. (1992). *Helping skills for middle school students*. Minneapolis, MN: Educational Media Corporation.

Myrick, R.D. & Sorenson, D.L. (1992). *Teaching helping skills to middle school students*. Minneapolis, MN: Educaitonal Media Corporation.

Painter, C. (1989). *Friends helping friends: A manual for peer counselors*. Minneapolis, MN: Educational Media Corporation.

Painter, C. (1989). *Leading a friends helping friends program*. Minneapolis, MN: Educational Media Corporation.

Paolitto, D.P. (1976). The effect of cross-age tutoring on adolescence: An inquiry with theoretical assumptions. *Review of Educational Research, 46*(2), 215-237.

Rauch, S.J. (1975). *Handbook for the volunteer tutor*. Newark, DE: International Reading Association.

Reardon, M.T. (1991). Effectiveness of peer counseling on high school students who failed tow or more classes in a nine-week quarter. *Peer Facilitator Quarterly, 8*(4), 9-14.

Resnick, H.S., & Gibbs, J. (1986). Types of peer program approaches. In *Adolescent peer pressure theory, correlates, and program implication for drug abuse prevention*. New York: Gordon Press.

Rogers, C.R. (1961, 1972). *On becoming a person*. Boston: Houghton Mifflin.

Rogers, C.R. (1962). The interpersonal relationship: The core of guidance. *Harvard Education Review, 32*, 416-429.

Rogers, C.R. (1980). *A way of being*. Boston: Houghton Mifflin.

Samuels, D., & Samuels, M. (1975). *The complete handbook of peer counseling*. Miami, FL: Fiesta Publishing Corp.

Sasso, G.M., et al. (1986). Peer tutoring versus structured interaction activities: Effects on the frequency and topography of peer initiations. *Behavioral Disorders, 11*(4), 249-259.

Schmidt, J.J. (1988). *Invitation to friendship*. Minneapolis, MN: Educational Media Corporation.

Sciacca, J. (1990). Research and evaluation: Evaluating peer helping programs. *Peer Facilitator Quarterly, 8*(2), 15.

Scott, S. (1985). *Peer pressure reversal*. Amherst, MA: Human Resource Development Press, Inc.

Shepherd, D.L. (1973). *Comprehensive high school reading methods*. Columbus, OH: Charles E. Merrill Publishing Company.

Sorenson, D.L. (1992). *Conflict resolution and mediation for peer helpers.* Minneapolis, MN: Educational Media Corporation.

Sprinthall, N.A., & Erickson, V.L. (1974). Learning psychology by doing psychology: Guidance through the curriculum. *Personnel and Guidance Journal, 52,* 396-405.

Swengel, E.M. (1991). Peer tutoring: Back to the roots of peer helping. *Peer Facilitator Quarterly, 8*(4), 28-32.

Thomas, E.L., & Robinson, H.A. (1977). *Improving reading in every class: A sourcebook for teachers.* Boston, MO: Allyn & Bacon, Inc.

Tindall, J.A. (1989). *Peer counseling: An in-depth look at training peer helpers,* (third edition). Muncie, IN: Accelerated Development, Inc.

Tindall, J.A. (1985). *Peer power, book 1: Becoming an effective peer helper, introductory program,* (second edition). Muncie, IN: Accelerated Development, Inc.

Tindall, J.A. (1989). *Peer power, book 2: Applying peer helper skills,* (second edition). Muncie, IN: Accelerated Development, Inc.

Tindall, J.A., & Gray H. (1974). Communication training study: A model for training junior high school peer counselors. *School Counselor, 22*(14), 107-112.

Tindall, J.A., & Salmon-White, S. (1990). *Peers helping peers program for the preadolescent: Student workbook.* Muncie, IN: Accelerated Development, Inc.

Tindall, J.A., & Salmon-White, S. (1990). *Peers helping peers program for the preadolescent: Leader manual.* Muncie, IN: Accelerated Development, Inc.

Topping, K. (1988). *The peer tutoring handbook: Promoting co-operative learning.* Cambridge, MA: Brookline Books.Topping, K. (1988). *The peer tutoring handbook: Promoting co-operative learning.* Cambridge, MA: Brookline Books.

Topping, K. (1989). Peer tutoring and paired reading: Combining two powerful techniques. *Reading Teacher, 42*(7), 488-494.

Topping, K., & Whiteley, M. (1990). Participant evaluation of parent tutored and peer tutored projects in reading. *Educational Research 32,* 14-32.

Varenhorst, B.B. (1983). *Real friends: Becoming the friend you would like to have.* New York: Harper Collins.

Code of Ethics for Peer Helpers National Peer Helpers Association

June, 1990

Peer Helpers shall be people of personal integrity. As a minimum, the NPHA believes the peer helpers Code of Ethics shall contain the following and be evidenced by a commitment to and pursuit of:

1. A philosophy which upholds peer helping as an effective way to address the needs and conditions of people.
2. The individual's right to dignity, self-development, and self-direction.
3. Supervision and support from professional staff while involved in the program.
4. The development of a nurturing personality which:
   - Reflects a positive role model and healthy lifestyle (i.e., development and observation of a set of norms which guide behavior while in the program).
   - Rejects the pursuit of personal power, elitist status, or gain at the expense of others.
   - Strives to exemplify the peer helping philosophy in all life situations.
5. Maintenance of confidentiality of information imparted during the course of program-related activities. While confidentiality is the norm, certain exceptions shall be referred immediately to the professional staff. These exceptions include the following:
   - Situations involving real or potential danger to the safety or well-being of the peer helper, helpee, or others.
   - Child abuse, sexual abuse, and other situations involving legal requirements of disclosure.
   - Severe family dysfunction, psychotic behavior, extreme drug or alcohol abuse, and any other problems beyond the experience and expertise of the peer helper.
6. Personal Safety. Peer helpers must recognize, report, and know techniques to deal with potential threats to their emotional or physical well-being.